CW00705391

First published in the UK by
New Cavendish Books
June 2003.

Publisher: Narisa Chakra
Design: Peter Cope
Photography: Richard Mann

ISBN: 1 872727 49 2

Printed and bound in Thailand by
Amarin Printing & Publishing [Plc] Co., Ltd.

New Cavendish Books
3 Denbigh Road
London W11 2SJ
Tel: 020 7229 6765
Fax: 020 7792 0027
email: narisa@newcavendishbooks.co.uk
www.newcavendishbooks.com

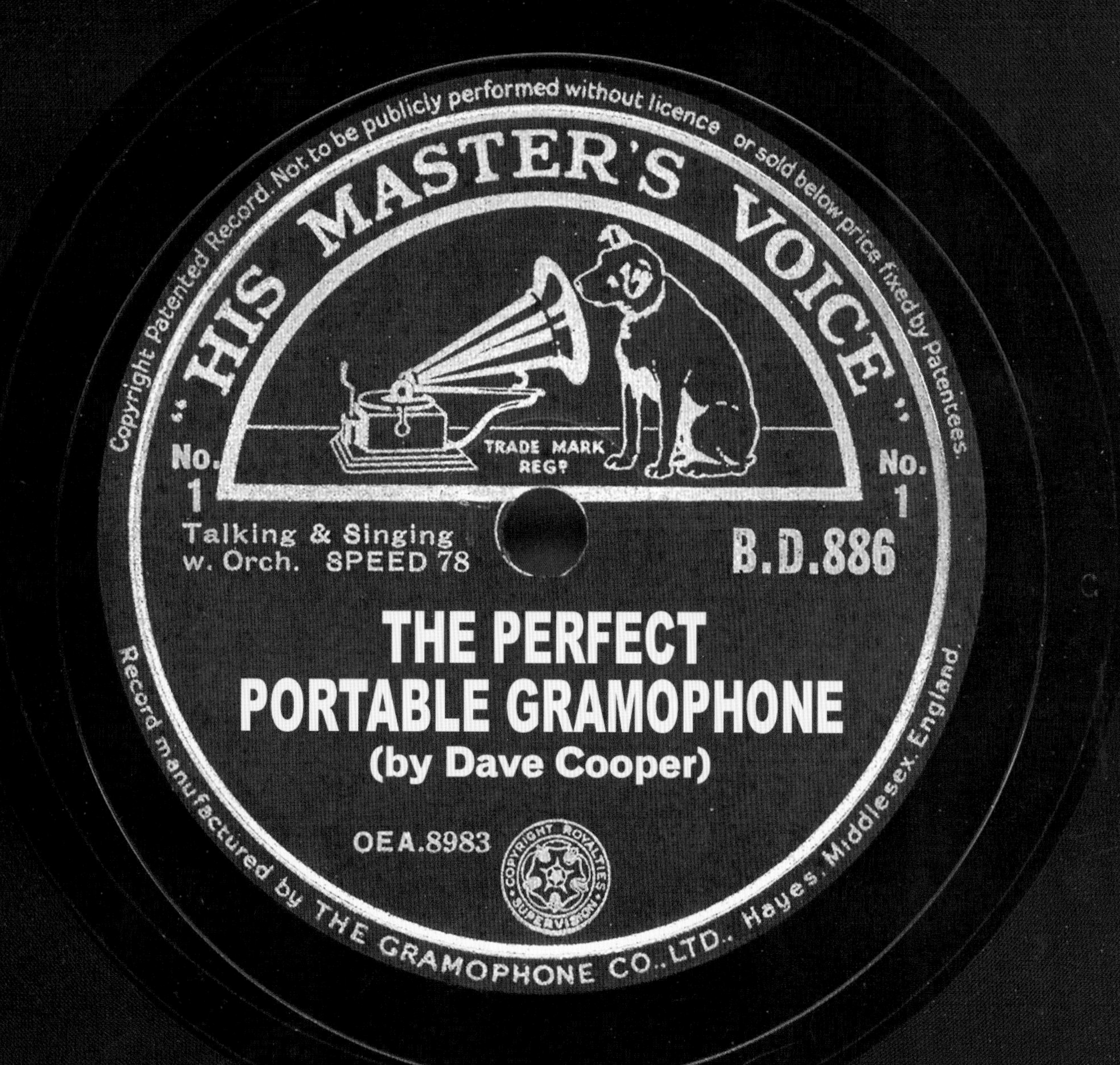

Copyright Patented Record. Not to be publicly performed without licence or sold below price fixed by Patentees.
"HIS MASTER'S VOICE"
TRADE MARK REGD
No. 1
No. 1
Talking & Singing
w. Orch. SPEED 78
B.D.886
THE PERFECT
PORTABLE GRAMOPHONE
(by Dave Cooper)
OEA.8983
COPYRIGHT ROYALTIES SUPERVISION
Record manufactured by THE GRAMOPHONE CO., LTD., Hayes, Middlesex, England.
OEA 8983

Acknowledgements

I would like to acknowledge the following people who were kind enough to share information and illustrations: Richard Buckley, Robin Edwards, Neil Gerty, John Gomer, Nick Hines, Steve Miller, Peter R Moore and Ken Priestley.

Additional thanks also to: Roger Thorne and Christopher Proudfoot of the City of London Phonograph and Gramophone Society, both acknowledged experts on His Master's Voice and the Gramophone Company, who offered valuable advice on drafts of the text, which was very important as so few written records appear to exist. I am particularly grateful to Roger who generously shared his time and extensive archives in order to clarify as far as possible a number of grey areas.

In addition, my appreciation to Ruth Edge of EMI Archives for her support of the project and for her introductory notes. The His Master's Voice trademark appears by kind permission of EMI Records Ltd.

To Rena David and Colin

Contents

From a postcard of His Master's Voice factories at Hayes, Middlesex, England c1930.

Foreword

There are people all over the world who collect both records and gramophones, and there are several very active societies dedicated to this particular field. The early machines sell at auction for considerable sums of money but portable gramophones are readily available, affordable and attractive – especially the coloured models.

    The EMI Archive receives many enquiries from the general public who wish to date their machines and obtain more information on their acquisitions. Unfortunately, there are few publications to which we can refer them, so I am particularly pleased to see this book in print.

From the back cover of His Master's Voice gramophone catalogue 1922.

Ruth Edge
Chief Archivist
EMI Music Archive

"His Master's Voice"

The Symbol
of
Supremacy

Introduction

There were always a number of 78-rpm records around the house for me to listen to as a child. Like many other families, our records were played on a radiogram in wall-to-wall mono, for this was the end of the 1950s and the age of high fidelity. Revolutionary new popular microgroove records played at 45 revolutions per minute, were only 7 inches in diameter, light in weight and most importantly were unbreakable with normal use. Early electric tone arms were on the heavy side, but were less likely to damage the records with a diamond or sapphire stylus!

78s were still available in the late 1950s and reproduction from later pressings was actually very good. 78s were generally made from brittle shellac and were much heavier and larger (popular records were 10 inches in size) than their replacements the 45rpm record. Some 78 records had been manufactured from 'unbreakable' materials back in the 1930s but the companies that made them were not in business for very long. During the War, records made for the US Forces (V Discs) were pressed in plastic. Unfortunately, steel needles and the heavy tone arms of the gramophone were not the best of marriages, especially when used on softer materials like plastic. By the late 1950s some record companies were pressing 78s in plastic again but time had moved on and soon 78 production ceased altogether in favour of the 45rpm.

Although I had a large selection of current music on 45s and LPs, I began collecting 78s as a child, to augment those in the family collection. Eventually, I bought my first gramophone, spotted hiding under a sofa in a used furniture shop whilst my mother was talking to the proprietor. It turned out to be a His Master's Voice model 101. I had never seen one like it before, a wind-up, spring driven gramophone in a suitcase! Despite the fact that it cost 30 shillings (£1. 10s or £1.50 in today's money), I just had to have it! I had many happy hours with it in the mid-1960s when I was nine or ten. It has remained my favourite gramophone.

If contemporary advertisements were correct then I was in famous company in owning and liking the 101. The 101 'club' included famous artists of the 1920s and 30s: Essie Ackland, contralto; Amelita Galli Curci, soprano; John Brownlee, baritone; Lilian Davies, soprano; Frieda Leider,

Far left: Record catalogues were issued annually. This one dates from 1933 and depicts composer/conductor Edward Elgar.

Above left: John Brownlee and his model 101.

Below left: Record cover featuring Russian operatic bass Fedor Chaliapin and his model 101.

soprano; Sergei Rachmaninoff, classical pianist and composer; Fedor Chaliapine, bass and Jack Hylton, band leader. There are famous pictures of the popular dance band vocalist Al Bowlly, using a model 101. I ceased collecting 78s as I grew older and discarded my gramophone. My work took me away from home for long periods and there were other distractions too.

I had my interest rekindled quite by accident when a series on BBC Radio about Al Bowlly was aired. From that, I started looking for Bowlly 78s and a machine to play them on. Eventually, I became the proud owner of a Decca 'Crescendo' portable gramophone, but it didn't satisfy my needs. I had to have the best – a His Master's Voice portable!

The first one came along in the shape of a model 102 in blue leatherette, and then a black model 101 like the one I owned so many years before. I had never heard of coloured 101s until someone I visited showed me a red version, which was conveniently for sale. As I collected the various coloured 101s, I found myself looking for as much information on them as I could find and it is this which forms the basis of this book, which not only celebrates the popular model His Master's Voice 101 but also the other more compact His Master's Voice portable gramophones.

Like me, some collectors prefer the 101 to the later model 102. This relates to its appearance and general tone (albeit perhaps limited in certain ranges). Discussions about the relative merits of each model and other makes still fill the occasional column in collector's magazines. What I like is the range of colours and styles of fitments that are generally more extensive on the model 101.

Imperial measurements appear in the text in keeping with the period. Because suppliers of replacement mica diaphragms and springs use metric sizes, these measurements are sometimes referred to. I am always interested in anything related to His Master's Voice portable gramophones – especially the 101, so if you have any information to offer, I will be pleased to hear from you.

Dave Cooper
August 2002

Part 1
Beginnings of a New Industry
(1888-1925)

Emile Berliner first demonstrated his (flat) disc gramophone in 1888. It was available as a toy in Europe in the early 1890s with 5-inch records. In 1895 the Berliner Gramophone Company produced serious entertainment on 7-inch records but gramophones were hand powered until Eldridge Johnson, an engineer from Camden, New Jersey, came up with a successful clockwork motor in 1896.

In 1897 William Barry Owen was sent to London by Berliner to establish a European gramophone trade. This was to protect patents, but also led to the creation of the Gramophone Company. Owen promoted and traded Berliner's records and Johnson's gramophones.

Berliner contacted his brother Joseph in Hanover, Germany with a view to building a factory for the manufacture of records to play on the trademark type gramophones sold from London. The Hanover plant became the Deutsche Grammophon Gesellschaft. Around this time, the famous His Master's Voice painting by Francis Barraud was adopted as the trademark for the Gramophone Company in Britain (in addition to the 'recording angel'). Johnson also used it for the Victor Talking Machine Company, created when he and Berliner merged their businesses in 1901. In Britain, the business became the Gramophone & Typewriter Company Limited in 1900, when in addition to gramophones, the Lambert Typewriter was sold. The typewriter was not a success. The business reverted to its earlier name of the Gramophone Company Limited in 1907.

The gramophone industry boomed. Record manufacturing plants were built in many countries, including France, Spain, Russia and India, to meet the growing demand. Victor traded in the Americas, Canada and the Far East (including Japan), while the Gramophone Company traded just about everywhere else! Recordings made by each company were shared under licence. The famous Hayes (Middlesex) factories were built in 1907, providing records and gramophones for the home and export markets stopping only during World War I to work on munitions.

In the beginning, buying recordings and record machines was a pastime for the elite rich. One of the most famous names to be persuaded to make records was the Australian soprano Nellie Melba, who insisted that her records bore her own distinctive label, which cost a guinea each (£1 1s 0d) – a huge price at the time. For that you

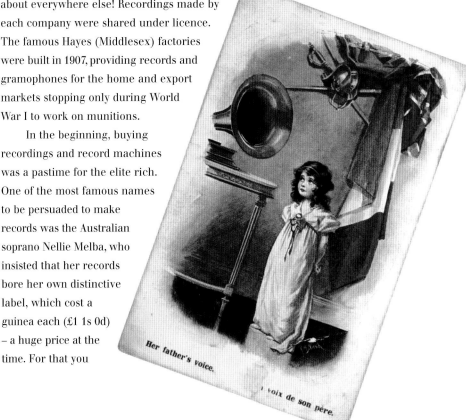

Below: A humorous British postcard lampooning the famous His Master's Voice trade name c1920.

Right: Record supplements were issued to promote new record releases every month and sometimes mid-monthly too.

Her father's voice.

voix de son père.

14

*Above: His Master's Voice
record supplement.*

had a record of poor sound quality, pressed on one side only and lasting for only three minutes. As more and more big names started to record, like Enrico Caruso the famous Italian operatic tenor, the gramophone became more popular. Double-sided records arrived around 1908. Record sales were high as more and more homes acquired gramophones.

Industrial recession during the 1920s forced Victor to provide the necessary financial investment to enable the Gramophone Company to stay in business. 'Electrical' recordings arrived in 1925 with the invention of the microphone, which greatly improved the sound range of recording. You can see references to 'electric' recordings on the labels of 78rpm records from this period. The Gramophone Company realised that its recording facilities at Hayes did not meet rapidly improving standards, so purchased number 3, Abbey Road, London NW8 and developed the property into what are now perhaps the most famous recording studios in the world. Abbey Road Studios opened in November 1931.

As time passed, gramophones and records reduced in price. Even so, His Master's Voice still had a wide price range for records for different types of music. Operatic records were often the most expensive and sometimes had more colourful labels. Even in 1927, these might cost up to 15

A record supplement c1930.

shillings each. The popular end of the range, a
ten-inch double sided record on the famous plum
coloured label, would cost 3 shillings. By 1930, as
the recession took hold, it had dropped to 2s 6d.
This record category included dance bands, singers
and comedians performing the popular songs of
the day. Movies with sound were introduced in
1927 and all record companies were swift to put
music featured from films or heard on radio onto
their records.

Together, the Victor Company in the United
States and the Gramophone Company in England
signed up most of the top artistes from all fields of
entertainment to record exclusively for them.

Having a cheaper range of records meant
that people on lower wages could afford them.
Often portable gramophones were bought in
preference to table or floor standing models,
which were more expensive. Only those earning
high salaries would be in a position to regularly
purchase the latest recordings. Sales of records
and machines dropped dramatically due to the
effects of the Depression around 1930.

The Columbia Company was the main
business rival to the Gramophone Company and
Victor. Columbia started out as a producer of
cylinders and phonographs in the United States,
but by the early 1920s, the British arm of the
Columbia Company had managed to purchase its

Postcard of a lady and a Columbia portable Model 109.

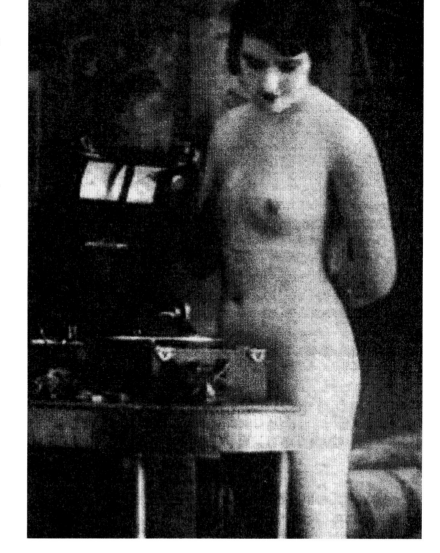

American parent company. Later, it was able to buy Carl Lindstrom, the big German company, giving Columbia ownership of the Parlophone and Odeon catalogues. Next, it acquired the French company Pathé with its international connections.

It was only because of a huge slump in the market that Columbia eventually agreed to merge with the Gramophone Company. However, times were hard and even a merger of two leading businesses started off as a disaster. Recovery took time and was only achieved after the new company, Electric and Musical Industries (EMI) reorganised to focus on radio, radiograms and cheaper (1s 6d) records at the popular end of the market.

The Portable Gramophone

The portable gramophone is only part of a range of models that included table and floor standing varieties designed for home use. Portables, referred to in this book, are those generally self-contained models requiring little if any setting up before use. Early gramophones were promoted as 'portable', but often required packing or unpacking into a separate case.

External horn gramophones were gradually replaced by 'hornless' models, where the sound was directed through the case, often past two doors

Record supplement
showing price reductions
September 1931.

Far left: Record supplement featuring Gracie Fields.

Left: Cover telling the story of Nipper.

Below: HMV 101 cover.

used to control volume. Contemporary leaflets sometimes referred to these machines as portable models. Comparing them with external trumpet models they undoubtedly were, but they usually required the removal or replacement of parts in transit. Not until the gramophone was enclosed in its own case with carrying handle, self contained ready for use upon lifting the lid, could a portable machine be considered truly portable.

Portable gramophones may have appeared as early as 1909. The Decca portable gramophone appeared in 1914, made by the company Barnett Samuel and Sons. It is remembered for being the most significant model of its kind in its day and popular with the forces fighting in the trenches during World War I. This machine had a bowl in the lid to reflect the sound from a short tone arm. The design continued into the 1920s on even larger and more expensive *Decca* models – the most important portable until the introduction of the His Master's Voice model 101. The Decca reflecting horn was called the 'Dulciflex'. Other similar types and makes were sent out to the troops, including the Apollo, shown on sets of postcards entertaining troops with the words of songs like *Take Me Back to Dear Old Blighty*.

'In England during the Great War, the cheap portable machine was all the rage and proved a boon to the soldiers, as it broke the monotony of their routine existence in the dug out. Popular patriotic songs were recorded and distributed in thousands.

The gramophone was encouraged by the military authorities of both sides, who looked upon it as a vital necessity.'
(From *Music on Record* by FW Gaisberg).

Left: Generic instruction leaflet for table and floor standing models.

Below: World War I postcard showing the Apollo portable as used in the trenches.

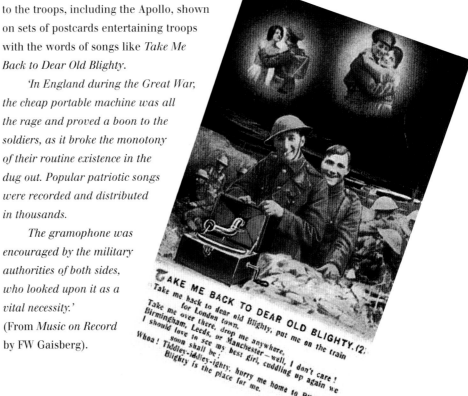

Part 2
Early His Master's Voice
Portable Gramophones
(1920-1925)

The first portable His Master's Voice model PAAO (portable version A in oak) appeared in 1920 selling at £15 0s 0d. A heavy and bulky machine, it could play a 10-inch record with the lid closed. When in the playing position, it looked much like a table model with a wax-finish oak cabinet and external fittings in oxidised copper. The tone arm fed into a crude internal horn partially blocked by the machine's motor, which was a standard vertical spring motor, the only concession to lightness being alloy castings instead of iron. It had doors across the grill at the mouth of the horn to control the volume, but more important, had a carrying handle to qualify it as a portable. In 1921, the price was reduced to £13 10s 0d – still expensive.

By 1922 came the PBO (portable version B in oak), which, when closed was slightly smaller due to a hinged motor-board, which lowered itself into the case when closed. The case was covered in leather-cloth in 1923. (This was given the model reference PBC portable version B in black. The letter C was used to refer to black cloth covering.) In 1924, the His Master's Voice portable took on the model number 105, with blackened nickel

His Master's Voice gramophone catalogue 1922.

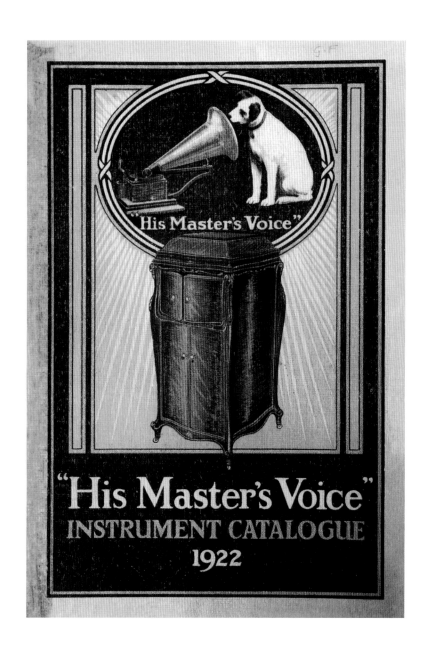

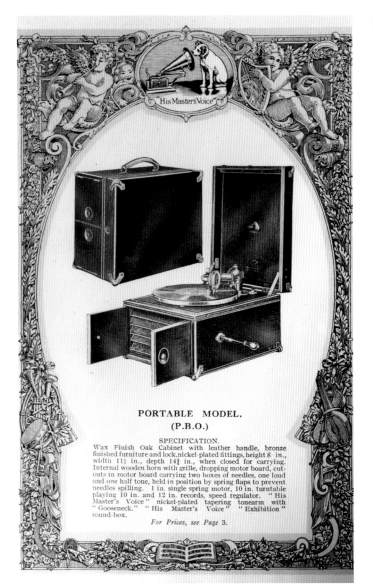

PORTABLE MODEL.
(P.B.O.)

SPECIFICATION.

Wax Finish Oak Cabinet with leather handle, bronze finished furniture and lock, nickel-plated fittings, height 8 in., width 11½ in., depth 14½ in., when closed for carrying. Internal wooden horn with grille, dropping motor board, cut-outs in motor board carrying two boxes of needles, one loud and one half tone, held in position by spring flaps to prevent needles spilling. 1 in. single spring motor, 10 in. turntable playing 10 in. and 12 in. records, speed regulator. "His Master's Voice" nickel-plated tapering tonearm with "Gooseneck." "His Master's Voice" "Exhibition" sound-box.

For Prices, see Page 3.

Left: His Master's Voice gramophone catalogue 1922 model PBO.

Above: His Master's Voice advertisement on the inside cover of contemporary magazines. It shows part of the 1923 range including the portable model.

fittings and a new price of £9 0s 0d. *The Voice,*
the Gramophone Company's monthly trade journal
remarked that the model 105 had become a mascot
for the English Rugby team in 1925.

His Master's Voice Model 100 (1924-1925)

It was only possible to make a truly portable
gramophone when the smaller horizontal single
spring motor was introduced. His Master's Voice's
model 100 was the result. The 100's sound system
was like the system discussed earlier in Decca
portable machines. The sound created by the
soundbox passed through the short gooseneck tone
arm and was reflected upwards from a metal well
in the base of the case. The sound then reflected
into the angle made by the record pocket in the lid.
The arm rose to the playing position when moved
to the right. When the machine was closed, the
tone arm sat in the sound well in its lower position.

The record pocket, an important feature on
the model 100, (and continued on the model 101),
was not offered by Decca or Columbia. It had two
supporting claws in addition to screws situated on
the lower corners on each side acting as hinges.
The ferrule[1] in the record pocket spindle hole did
not appear in the first 100s or on tropical models.
The catch[2] was small by comparison with later
models, smaller even than those used on the later
His Master's Voice 99 gramophone, which had a
number of other small fittings. The speed control
plate (under the turntable) was also small. The

23

Top left: Model PBC doors open.
Above: Model PBC doors closed.
Left: Model PBC tin and socket

Top left: Model 100 open handle in clips.

Above: Model 100 inside under motorboard internal plate.

Top: Model 100 Exhibition soundbox and arm.

Left: Model 100 in teak.

Model 100 open ready for use.

10-inch turntable had no raised rim, so the felt mat covered up to its edge. The three winding handle clips[3] sat diagonally near the tone arm.

The model 100 was available from June 1924 to October 1925 and it is known that 6,803 were sold in Britain. *The Voice* reported that the Model 100 'made a great hit' in Harrods, London.

Model	His Master's Voice 100
Colours	Black (or Tropical version in teak. Not UK)
Soundbox	His Master's Voice Exhibition (43mm mica diaphragm)
Motor	No. 400 (425)
Escutcheon	Style 1[4]
Fittings	All bright nickel
Identifying plate	None, but see comments
Winding handle	Style 1[5]
Carrying handle	Style 1[6]

Notes for the collector

Note the sprung self-closing needle containers in the right hand corner of the lid. A small black plate with white numbering sits inside the case on some model 100s. The illustrated black model 100 is numbered 4853. A friend's machine is 15986. I have examined another one, numbered 3705. Not all 100s have this plate nor are the numbers always painted white. The plate is similar to those on other gramophone models such as table varieties. On these, the plate is partially hidden behind the doors and is attached to the slats over the mouth of the internal horn. I suspect that the numbers are simply serial numbers.

Ferrules were not fitted to the tropical versions of portable machines, specially built for the Eastern market. The top and bottom of the teak 100 case was flat. On teak 101s, panels were used, strengthened with screws presumably to allow for the effect of climatic heat on the wood.

Left: Model 100 as advertised c1925.

Above: Model 101 trademark 1 patent applied for.

Part 3
His Master's Voice
Model 101
(1925-1931)

A record cover boasted in 1926 that the portable model C101 (was) ' *...the greatest advance ever made in the science of musical reproduction ... this new Gramophone is exactly like any standard His Master's Voice instrument. The secret of its amazing realism lies in the design of a special tone chamber inside the cabinet, and a new soundbox. This result has been attained in His Master's Voice laboratories by the application of an entirely new scientific principle of sound amplification.'*

Above: Model 101 Glasgow ivorine dealer's plate.

Model 101. Second version.

Model 101 ready to play.

Model	His Master's Voice 101
Dimensions	Closed. 16¼" x 5½" x 11¼" (as model 100). The case of the teak or tropical version is slightly larger (and considerably heavier)
Colours	Black (Colour code: C101)
	Brown, Crocodile/Brown (Col. code: BR101)
	Blue, Crocodile/Blue (Col. code LB101)
	Grey, Crocodile/Grey (Col. code G101)
	Red (Colour code R101)
	Green (Colour code V101)
	Red Leather (Colour code RL101)
	Teak (tropical version) (Col. code unknown)
Price	Black – £7.0s.0d
	Brown, Crocodile/Brown – £8.10s.0d
	Blue, Crocodile/Blue – £8.10s.0d
	Grey, Crocodile/Grey – £8.10s.0d
	Red – £8.10s.0d
	Green – £8.10s.0d
	Red Leather – £11.0s.0d
	Teak (tropical version) – Price unknown
Soundbox	His Master's Voice No.4 (Mica fronted-54mm)
Tone Arm	Narrow bore 'swan neck' shape
Motors	Single horizontal spring
Turntable	10 inch

The Model 101 (front winding version) from an advertisement c1927.

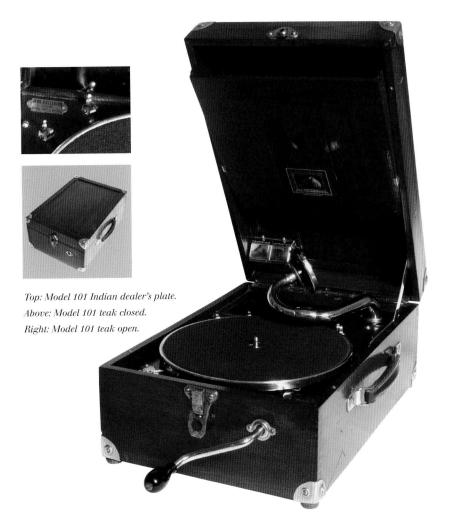

Top: Model 101 Indian dealer's plate.
Above: Model 101 teak closed.
Right: Model 101 teak open.

All black machines had cellulose polished motor boards and brown felt covered turntables. Cellulose was used for most His Master's Voice cabinets from 1924. Coloured 101s had matching leather-cloth on their motor boards, measuring approximately 10 inches x 8½ inches. On the first front wind version of the 101, the edge of the tone arm board abutting the motor board was beaded. The winding handle clips on the two front wind model 101s were not well positioned and it is unusual to find all three complete, no matter how careful the original owner may have been. The winding handle was held diagonally on the tone arm board. The second front wind model (with new corner needle drawer) was shown in the 1926 His Master's Voice gramophone catalogue. On the later side winding machines, the winding handle was held parallel to the sides of the case, until a new stronger clip and socket system was introduced, housed in the machine's lid.

Turntable felts on coloured machines usually came in a similarly coloured felt to the leather-cloth of the case. There are two brown crocodile cloth machines but I am of the opinion that one of them is the model advertised as 'grey crocodile' cloth, as it is a paler brown than its counterpart and has a pale beige turntable felt. The mouth of the internal horn is also sprayed grey. I have encountered only two of these machines and so far have not met anyone, dealer or collector who recalls ever seeing a clearly identifiable grey

Left: Model 101
grey leather
open and closed.

Above: Model 101
red leather
open and closed.

crocodile-cloth 101. Even the later grey leatherette version is uncommon. It is a peculiar colour, not really a standard grey at all, more of a buff colour, that despite its general unattractiveness, was also used unchanged on 102s.

The red leather version had gilt fittings. Its shade was ox-blood and was complemented by a deep pinkish red turntable felt. Later, red leather-covered machines were much brighter in colour. However, there were some differences in the hue of coloured leather-cloths, possibly explained by variations in the batches of material or fading due to age. One brown leather-covered machine with gilt fittings exists – a one-off used in a window display from the Oxford Street HMV shop in the 1920s! It's current owner (sadly not the author) has kindly allowed its picture to be included in the book. It should be noted that the original owner

Top: Model 101 brown leather with gilt fittings closed.

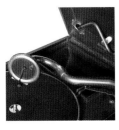

Above: Model 101 no. 4 soundbox.

Left: Model 101 brown leather with gilt fittings ready for use.

Right: Model 101 with winding handle stowed.

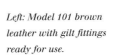

had the machine 'modernised' by the factory to add the new auto brake and winding handle clips and socket arrangement also in gilt.

Although the His Master's Voice 101 was one of the most commercially successful gramophones, much of the contemporary information about it appears not to have survived. For example, we may never know who designed any of the portable models, nor do we know exactly how many were made, other than that the London branch of the Gramophone Company sold around 220,000 101s between October 1925 and July 1931. This would suggest somewhere in the region of 500,000 sales worldwide – a staggering amount considering that the Gramophone Company was not noted for making low priced machines.

On an average wage during the 1920s period of around £3 9s 0d per week for labourers and £4 10s 0d for craftsmen, it is no wonder that some customers took advantage of buying gramophones 'on terms'.

With the wholesale price of £5 6s 8d for the black 101 (shown in a letter to dealers dated 23 October 1925) there was a great deal of money made, despite relatively small profits per machine. By comparison, earlier portable models are known to have had home sales of less than 2,000 each. The 101 was a market leader and the good publicity it received had obviously boosted sales. Retail outlets were quick to put their own trade plates on them, selections of which appear in this book.

Top: Model 101 early no. 4 soundbox and arm.

Middle: Model 101 gilt no. 4 soundbox and arm.

Below: Model 101 Second no. 4 soundbox and arm.

Factory workers assembling 101s in 1928. Note the huge numbers of gramophones at various stages of completion and that some teams are working on deluxe models on the same bench.

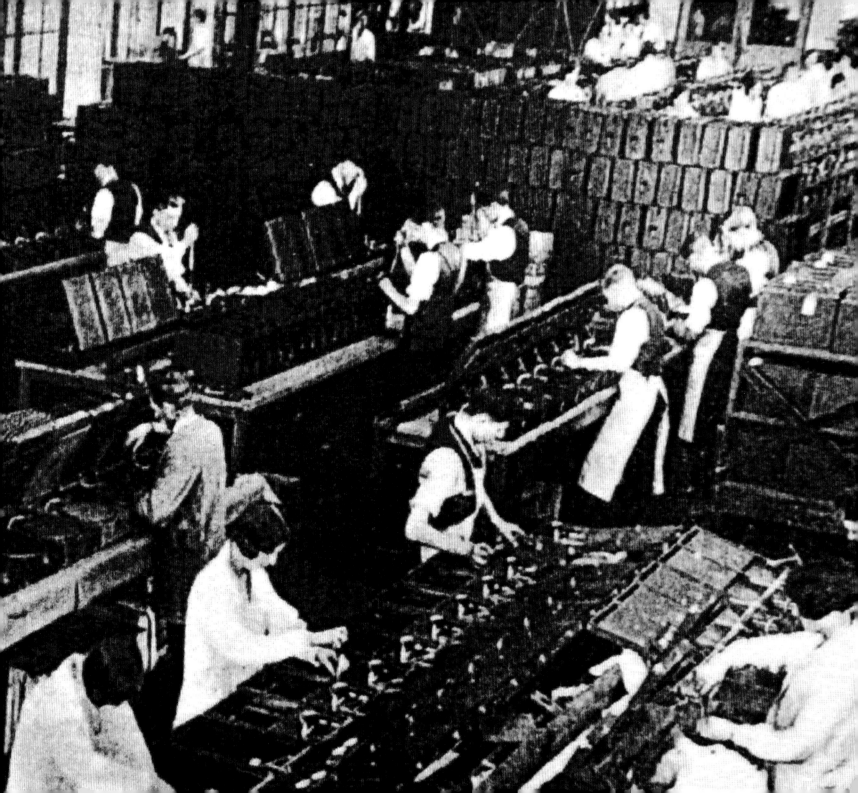

Model 101 blue crocodile open and closed.

Obviously some colours were more popular than others. Naturally, black 101s were the most popular, because they were less costly! Blue was next, if you base your assessment on the number you see for sale today.

The editor of *The Gramophone* magazine, Compton Mackenzie, reported on the model 101 in the November 1925 edition, after visiting the Hayes factory. *'It is not quite the thing for the editor of* The Gramophone *to say, but I really do feel rather sorry for other portables.'*

As you can see from the illustrations, the early 101 was quite closely related to the 100. The case was the same, so was the motor, the winding handle and the needle containers, although they were repositioned. The only real change was the sound system, including the shape and position of the tone arm.

The Exhibition soundbox had been in use since around 1903, but was not suitable for the new electric recordings. A new soundbox, the no. 2, had replaced the Exhibition on the cabinet models, but this too was replaced by the no. 4. (The no. 3 soundbox never saw the light of day). The no. 4 soundbox, used on the model 101, was designed to handle the wider sound frequency range of electric recordings introduced in 1925. Early boxes were identified in writing on the back-plate, visible through the mica diaphragm.

The tone arm was connected to an internal horn, which wound in a clockwise direction around

Left: Model 101
brown crocodile
open and closed.

Above: Model 101
grey crocodile
open and closed.

the space filled by the motor. The horn's mouth ended in the far left corner of the machine's case, from where the sound projected upwards to be deflected by the angle made by the lid. (The mouths of the internal horns were painted an appropriate colour to the case). The volume and tone of the machine was far superior to the performance of other portable gramophones of the period. The 101 innovations were eventually copied by most other manufacturers, including Decca and Columbia, on their successful portable models.

In June 1927, the Gramophone Company issued a leaflet on de-luxe portable gramophones, similar to the pages of the 1927/8 His Master's Voice instrument catalogue featuring colour-tinted pictures of all the coloured 101s available at the time. (Black, red leather, blue, grey, and brown crocodile cloth finish with 'nickel gloss' fittings.) The leaflet showed each machine set against a crocodile finish background.

The Voice remarked in 1926, that a portable model 101 was sold to Princess Ileana of Rumania and in August 1927, proclaimed *'Today the finest lady in the land can travel unashamed with her gramophone, for it is a thing of beauty. She travels luxuriously with the whole Covent Garden Orchestra tucked away in her blue crocodile valise.'*

Record supplements were issued monthly and sometimes mid-monthly to announce new record releases, this one featuring Leopold Stokowski. (February 1931)

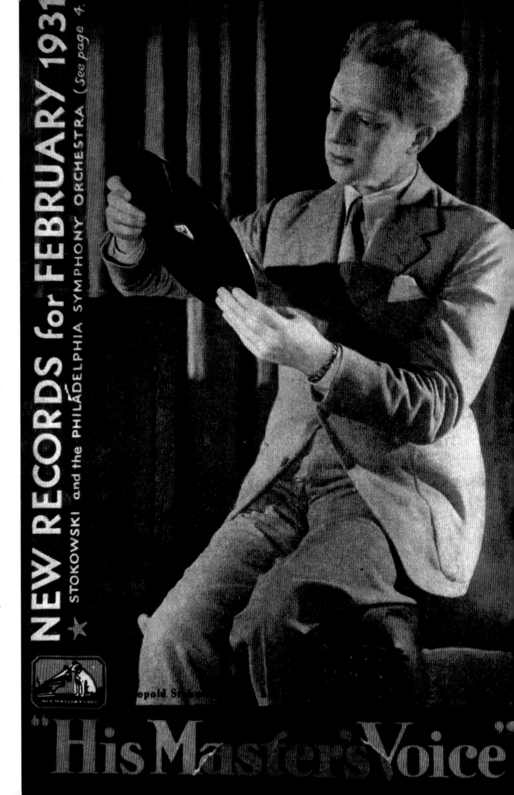

Sometimes, identification plates used on the 101 have the model number 101 followed by a letter. I tried to identify the function of these letters and whether they were related to the date of manufacture. The task was made all the more difficult by the fact that early machines did not have an identification plate at all. The first machine to do so carried the number 101E. Only letters G, H, J, L and N followed. Some letters may have been allocated to export models.

Perhaps, the letter, when used, could have referred to batches of machines for the purpose of ordering spare parts accurately when, for example, variations to the motor were introduced. The identification plates remind the owner of the machine to quote the model number for spare parts. It is possible that the letters have no useful meaning at all on 101s. A parts list dated February 1931 refers to the model 101N which had the later 270 motor and chromium fittings.

In later years and later models, a letter referred to a minor design modification. It could have been as simple a change as the introduction of metal corners (or shields). This innovation helped ease the job of the assembler in the factory by hiding awkward joins in the leather-cloth on the outer casing.

'Dancing on the lawn' – how the Gramophone Company saw their model 101 customers! I wonder how many purchasers actually had the free time or a lawn! (1928).

THE VOICE

A MONTHLY REVIEW PUBLISHED BY THE GRAMOPHONE COMPANY, LTD., 363–367, OXFORD STREET, LONDON, W.1, IN THE INTEREST OF BETTER AND GREATER BUSINESS FOR THEIR DEALERS AND THEMSELVES

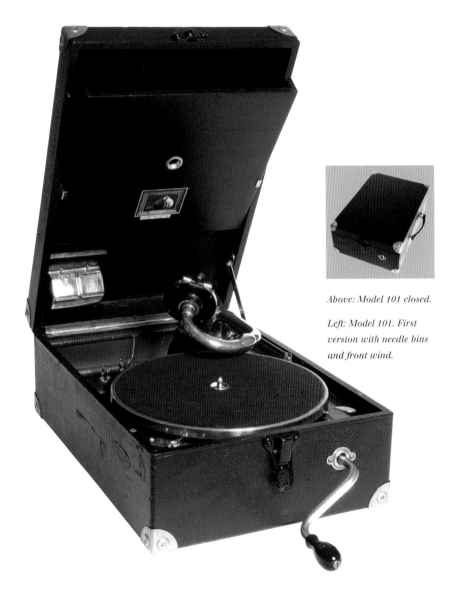

Above: Model 101 closed.

*Left: Model 101. First
version with needle bins
and front wind.*

Letters placed in front of the model number, for
example C101, relate to the colour of the case;
in this example the colour would be black. Colour
codes for the whole range are shown above.

There were two versions of the identification
plate when it changed from ivorine to metal. On
one, the text was in English, French and German.

All of the British and American companies in
Germany were seized by the German State during
World War I and put up for sale; so Polyphon
Musikwerke AG in Leipzig, eventually purchased
the German branch of the Gramophone Company.
Thus, after World War I, the His Master's Voice
trademark in Germany belonged to new owners
so, for export to Germany, the brand name was
Electrola. The Electrola Company was started in
Berlin in 1926 and 101s were available under that
name and transfer. Even the soundbox was marked
'Electrola no. 4'. I have seen a black example of one
as described, with a German dealer's trade plate.

The Gramophone Company did not always
use the most straightforward numbering systems,
so it is unwise to assume that the first 101 was
considered the 101A by His Master's Voice! Version
101A may have been the first version following the
original for example. However, I tried to identify
the machines in alphabetical order from A-N. If we
accepted the first incarnation of the 101 as model
101A, the 'version' might read:

Model	His Master's Voice 101A
Production date	From Autumn 1925
Colours	Black (Tropical version Teak)
Motors	No. 400
Escutcheon	Style 1[4]
Catch or lock	Style 2[7]
Fittings	Bright nickel plate
Identifying plate	None
Winding handle	Style 1[5]
Carrying handle	Style 1[6]

Notes for the collector

Self-closing needle containers on the 101A as the 100, but positioned in the left corner of the lid.

Rubber feet not fitted to the bottom case shields.

No provision for Tungstyle needle tins.

Inside of the record pocket in the lid of the case often not finished with leather-cloth. The machine had the thick frame trademark transfer.

In regard to model 100 and 101 versions of the 400 motor, there is a difference in the shape of governor weights. The pressure plate is at the opposite end of the 100-governor shaft. 101 governors have an extra tooth or web on the worm.

The above information was based on examination of several early 101s and should be acceptable to collectors as accurate.

Some machines were assembled with a mixture of fittings to utilise old parts that were in the factory. The 1930 His Master's Voice instrument catalogue showed an earlier 101 than that actually on sale at the time. (The same picture also appears on some His Master's Voice record covers.)

Through *The Voice*, dealers were encouraged to promote the portable gramophone's potential. *'The portable is a delightful companion at the picnic, on the river, between sets of tennis and for that new popular pastime, the dance on the lawn.'* (I wonder how many working people were in the position to enjoy any of those activities in the late 1920s!).

Portable models as used in the countryside.

"TAKE IT WITH YOU"

The big sell continued – 1928: *'When last year de-luxe portables were introduced, their charming colours made an immediate appeal and they should not be forgotten, especially when your enquiries are from members of the fair sex.'*

In 1930, the editor announced a new motto for the spring and summer trade: *'Every car owner (is potentially) a portable owner to meet the growing family 'habit' of weekend car journeys.'*

The Gramophone Company made nearly all the parts for its machines. Only locks, catches, and carrying handles were bought in. These were supplied from firms such as Beddoe & Cheney. Ironically, locks and carrying handles are the parts of a His Master's Voice portable gramophone most likely to rust, as they are external items and not plated on brass like most other parts.

Order of Changes to the Model 101

The first changes to the 101 appeared around the autumn of 1926. The escutcheon[9] and winding handle[10] changed to Style 2. (The crank of the Style 1 winding handle had a deeper throw and the machine had to be placed on a raised level for winding. The Style 2 handle was not much better.) A Tungstyle needle clip[11] (Style 1) was introduced.

Even though the model 101 was a commercial success, it was not without its problems. A new right-hand corner needle drawer replaced the two needle bins held in the lid

Model 101 dealer's plate: Wallace Harris.

Model 101 blue closed.

Model 101 blue ready to use.

41

42

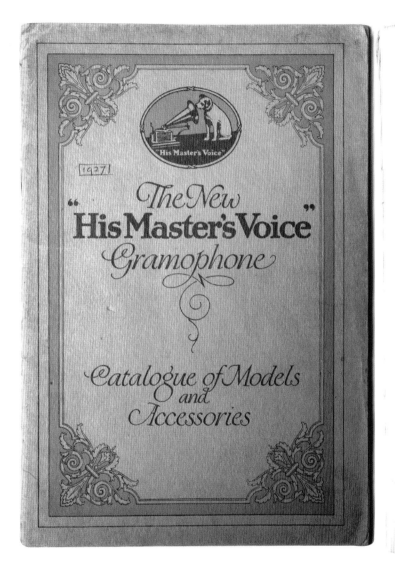

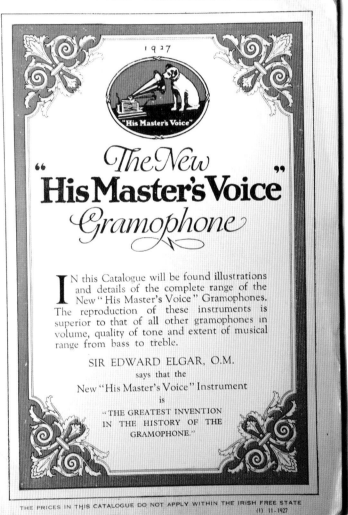

His Master's Voice 1927
gramophone catalogue
cover and inside page.

of the machine (carried over from the model 100). These were abandoned due to complaints of vibration as a record was played. The carrying handle clips required screws of different lengths, due to the position of the new needle drawer.

Under the motor board of some of the 'new' 101s were signs of the forthcoming side angle wind escutcheon shown as cut-aways in the supporting battens. The new side-winding versions probably arrived late in 1926 or early 1927. Rubber feet were incorporated into the shields on the bottom of the case.[12]

The winding handle changed to Style 3[15] and this was the first side-winding machine with the winding handle at an angle, which meant that the machine could be wound anywhere flat. The Style 2 Tungstyle needle tin clip[16] was also introduced at this time.

Coloured machines arrived in summer 1927. The colours on offer were black leather-cloth, blue, brown or grey crocodile cloth and red leather. The brown crocodile cloth was a beautiful chestnut colour with a lighter brown turntable felt to the one on the black machine's turntable. The red leather version had gilt fittings inside and out.

It should be emphasised that the appearance of the 101s in crocodile cloth generally differed between the inside and outside of the case. On the outside, the veins of the cloth are clearly seen. On the inside, the cloth seems darker as the veins are filled with colour.

Model 101 dealer's plate: Ludlow.

Above: Model 101 brown closed.

Right: Model 101 brown ready to use.

43

THE NEW "HIS MASTER'S VOICE" GRAMOPHONE

PORTABLE   MODEL 101

Height (closed), 11¼ ins. ; Width, 5¾ ins. ; Length, 16¼ ins.
Internal Fittings : Nickel Gloss Finish.   External Fittings : Oxidized.

New "His Master's Voice" Internal Horn, Ball Bearing Tone Arm and No. 4 Sound Box. Cabinet of light construction, covered with black leather waterproof cloth, fitted with leather carrying handle and metal corners and rubber non-slipping feet on base. Equipped with improved single spring motor, 10 inch turntable, playing records up to 12 ins. in diameter, graduated speed regulator. Pivoted needle bowl and spring clip for "Tungstyle" Needle Tin. Provision is made for carrying 6 records in lid.

£7   0   0

2

THE NEW "HIS MASTER'S VOICE" GRAMOPHONE

DE LUXE PORTABLE MODEL

Height (closed), 11¼ ins. ; Width, 5¾ ins. ; Length, 16¼ ins.
Gold Plated Fittings.

New "His Master's Voice" Internal Horn, Ball Bearing Tone Arm and No. 4 Sound Box. Cabinet of light construction, covered with red leather, fitted with leather carrying handle and metal corners and rubber non-slipping feet on base. Equipped with improved single spring motor, 10 inch turntable, playing records up to 12 ins. in diameter, graduated speed regulator. Pivoted needle bowl and spring clip for "Tungstyle" Needle Tin. Provision is made for carrying 6 records in lid.

£11   0   0

3

His Master's Voice gramophone
catalogue 1927, black leatherette version.

Deluxe red leather
with gold fittings version.

His Master's Voice
gramophone catalogue, 1927.
Blue crocodile leatherette version.

His Master's Voice
gramophone catalogue, 1927.
Brown crocodile leatherette version.

His Master's Voice
gramophone catalogue, 1927.
Grey crocodile leatherette version.

The escutcheon changed to Style 3.[13] There was a plate[14] attached to the top lid, which covered the winding hole when the case was closed. The inside fittings were finished in nickel; outside fittings were nickel on coloured machines and blackened nickel on black machines.

The escutcheon developed into to Style 4[17] and a new spring-loaded carrying handle Style 2[18] was called the 'Pakawa'. This was a more comfortable handle to use and lasted beyond the demise of the 101, on models 102 and 99 and were probably the first of the 'bought in' carrying handles. I have no information about their supplier. The escutcheon cover plate was discontinued.

The lock changed from Style 2[7] to Style 3[8]. The first identification plate[20] appeared and the new trademark with His Master's Voice above it replaced the 'patent pending', large framed transfer.

By late 1928, the crocodile cloth was replaced by morocco grain leather-cloth. A new colour (red leather-cloth) appeared. More importantly a new

46

Model 101 red open.

Top: Model 101 red open with handle in lid.

Above centre: Model 101 red closed.

Above: Model 101 dealer's plate: Blackpool.

motor, the no. 59 was used. This had a longer main spring and provided more power and ran longer, as well as a metal cover, which kept out dust.

By January 1929, green leather-cloth was introduced. The brown cloth changed to a much darker shade than previously when reintroduced in September 1929. The escutcheons were either the style 4[17] with a style 5[21] back-plate or a style 5[21] front and back plate. Old style 1[20] identification plates were used up and superseded by the style 2 plate[22]. Some machines of this period had both a style 2 and a metal plate[23] – others carried the metal plate only. The locks changed first to style 4[24] then to style 5[25]. There were two versions of the metal plate used to identify the version of the machine.

Eventually, the style 5 escutcheon took over and only the metal identification plate was used. Later, the style 5 lock was replaced by the style 6 version[26].

A 'tri-language' version of the metal plate[27] became the most commonly used identification plate and the Tungstyle needle tin clip style 3[28] was introduced.

The auto brake arrived which stopped the turntable on the eccentric run-out groove on His Master's Voice and Zonophone records of the period. The manual brake was made redundant and was no longer found. Telltale pinpricks, where an assembler would have previously screwed the part into the motor board are occasionally seen. New, stronger winding handle clips[30] were put into the

Above: Model 101 green closed.
Right: Model 101 open.

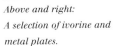

Above and right:
A selection of ivorine and
metal plates.

48

inside of the lid. (There was no room on the motor board.) The second metal identification plate was replaced by a third ivorine plate[31].

    An unmarked motor replaced the no. 59 motor around 1930, (actually motor no. 271C), found on the first 102s. The fittings changed from nickel plate to chromium. The trademark and His Master's

Top: Model 101
chrome no. 4
soundbox and arm.

Above: Model 101
blue chrome closed.

Model 101
in chrome
ready to play.

Voice wording reduced in size to that seen on later His Master's Voice portables, such as the 102 and 99. The turntable felts on these later machines varied slightly in colour to earlier 101s and these shades continued on new portable models. Another escutcheon was used on these late 101s – style 6[32]. The catch/lock moved to style 7[33], which was also used on the first 102s. Also, the motor-board on black models was now of a clamped, rather than laminated, construction. Various combinations of 59/270 motors with nickel or chromium fittings have been observed. *The Voice* printed a report in the June/July 1926 edition (Volume X Nos 6-7) headed *Boom in Portables*. It confirmed a crucial advantage of music at picnics.

A propos the portable, Mr Miller of Cambridge sends us this description from an undergraduate: *'The tone arm conveys the music to the place in which one puts the sandwiches.'*

Other Stories about the Model 101 taken from *The Voice* include:

The Perils Of A Portable, 1929

A portable bought in October 1926, was calculated to have played 10,000 records in its first eight months of its career by a Cambridge undergraduate; it survived splashes on the river and being played on a sandy beach; it travelled frequently on the back of a motor cycle quite unaffected by the vibration; it survived a train wreck in Spain (without even breaking a record in its 'pocket'); it endured temperatures of 100ºF to 20º of frost during travels.

'On the river' – promoting the de luxe range of the Model 101, August 1927.

Introducing a new Portable Model

Height (closed) 11½", width 9", length 16½". Fitted with leather carrying handle and metal corners, and rubber non-slipping feet on base. Plays records up to 12".

Price in red leather with gold-plated fittings - - £11 : 0 : 0

Price in blue, brown or grey crocodile cloth - - £8 : 10 : 0

(These prices do not apply to the Irish Free State.)

THE new "His Master's Voice" de luxe Portable Models will appeal particularly to those who desire a portable gramophone of exclusive design and distinguished appearance. They are made in several charming colours, and may be obtained either in red leather, or in grey, blue or brown crocodile cloth. The sound chamber is designed to give a depth of tone unobtainable in any other portable gramophone.

Ask your dealer to show you

The NEW "His Master's Voice" de Luxe Portable Gramophone

THE GRAMOPHONE COMPANY, LTD.
OXFORD STREET —— LONDON, W. 1.

"His Master's Voice"

De luxe Model 101 advertisement, c1927.

Great Performance!

Also from *The Voice*, 1929: *It is not usual to play a portable model in a large hall. At a recent recital given to an audience of over 500 in the Town Hall (Tavistock), this was done. Not as part of the recital, but as an 'extra' and an experiment, record B. 5637 (The Wedding of the Painted Doll, Jack Hylton and his Orchestra) was played on a portable. It could be heard clearly in every part of the hall.*

JACK HYLTON'S PORTABLE

"Although the boys are always with me I wouldn't be without my "His Master's Voice" Portable for worlds" says Jack Hylton, whose Portable bears eloquent evidence of its popular owner's travels.

Snake charmer

Mr LS Buckner, a South Indian coffee planter, tells how a His Master's Voice red leather portable charmed a huge cobra.

As deadly cobras appeared close to his bungalow, Mr Bucknall secured the services of a snake charmer and a native assistant. Their first catch was a cobra over 6 feet long, which had been known to be on the plantation for a dozen years. When its poison fangs had been extracted, the monster was dropped ten yards away from the gramophone, on which was being played My Blue Heaven, *as recorded on a Wurlitzer organ by Jesse Crawford.*

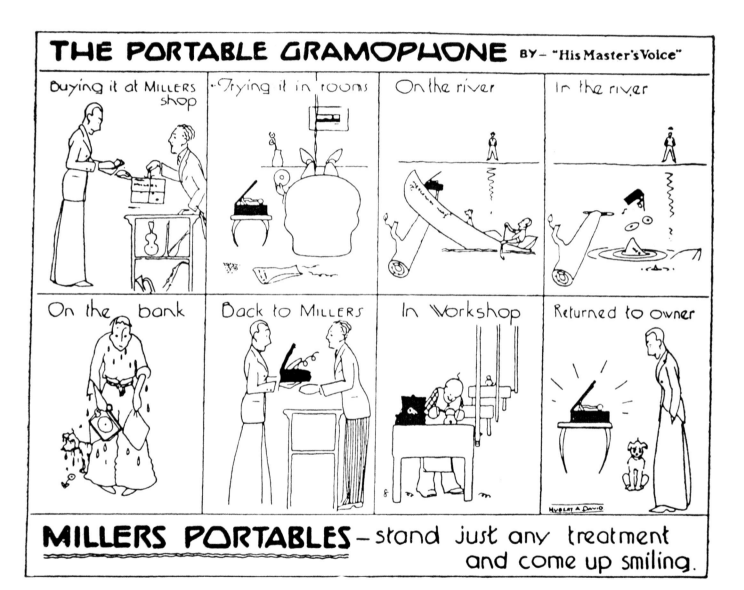

51

Millers portables.

Times have changed! After letting the cobra listen to a red leather de luxe, it was made into a pair of shoes.
The Voice 1929

The reptile at once crawled to the portable and raised its head, fascinated by the music, making no attempt to escape. When the music stopped, the cobra lay flat on the ground but rose again when the record was replayed.

After the performance the big cobra was killed and its skin used to make a pair of shoes for Mr Bucknall's mother. (*The Voice* 1929).

The Explorer
The His Master's Voice portable and records is accompanying the Mawson Antarctic Expedition. (The Voice 1929).

Stop Thief!
It was wryly amusing to find a report in the magazine The Gramophone *dated April 1928, that described a burglary on March 6 at Messrs. KG Clarke of Ilford. Various machines were taken, all His Master's Voice, and serial numbers were provided. The gramophones included a model 202, a table grand model 127 and a model 103, all in oak. 'Impecunious gramophiles are still busy breaking into the treasure houses' the article ran. 'The takings indicated the presence of connoisseurs.' Also in the haul was a grey crocodile cloth portable no. 8741.*

I know it was a long time ago, but who acquired the 101 – I wonder if indeed it still survives. I would love to know whether the machines were ever recovered.

His Masters Voice in other countries

Left: South African cover.

Below: Tungstyle needles advertisement (French cover).

Below left: La Voce del Padrone (Italian advertisement).

Part 4
Developing New Portables
(1927-1931)

Long before the demise of the 101 and the
introduction of models 102 and 99 in 1931, the
Gramophone Company was looking to produce
better portable gramophones (and table models)
that were no more expensive to purchase. The
sister company, Victor had introduced a range of
what they called 'orthophonic' gramophones
whose principles the Gramophone Company were
reluctant to adopt. In 1927, a representative from
the Gramophone Company visited Victor at its
factory in Camden, New Jersey and provided a
report. Victor had developed an 'orthophonic'
soundbox called the no. 5 in 1925. It used an
aluminium alloy diaphragm in place of the mica
diaphragm of earlier soundboxes. This was a die
cast soundbox, which Victor had outsourced due
to costs and a tool room with a huge backlog of
work. The subcontractors, the Doehler Company,
claimed that they could produce the soundboxes
cheaper and better than those seen in England.
However, Victor received complaints about
'orthophonic' gramophones and in particular, the
excessive noise emitted from the no. 5 soundbox.
The noise was reduced considerably by the use of
a felt pad held by a pressed outer cover.

    A soundbox with this modification came back
to England and work began to produce a suitable

Promoting the virtues of the portable through the summer, July 1929.

His Master's Voice version. The task was fraught with difficulties. By February 1928, tests proved that an adjustment problem in the no. 5 soundbox was causing a 'buzz' that was not easy to eliminate. Finding a solution to the buzzing soundbox was described as *'commercially the most important job we have on hand'*.

There was discontent with the motor in use, mainly due to an irregular noise, which the factory inspectors referred to as 'scroop'.

His Master's Voice looked at Victor models for inspiration. They regularly tested their products for performance, weight and finish, against other manufacturers such as Columbia and Decca. By August 1928, it was decided to have new models ready for the following year, allowing time for the study of production methods. As part of the process, machines from Victor and other major competitors were examined. The Victor machines *'were not liked'*, but their policy of producing two types of portable similarly built, using the same tooling, was taken forward.

Left: All metal prototype model open ready for use.

Below: Prototype closed.

Bottom: All metal prototype with sloping turntable.

55

One portable would be a redesign of the 101 with a no. 5 soundbox and the other a cheaper version.

The company decided not to use existing Victor models or copy other leading portables for their new lines. In January 1929, at variance with their stated policy, the factory was asked to build three prototypes, aimed at the retail price of £7, £5, and £4. As it transpired, none of these became the models 102 and 99 that we now know. The £4 model, an all metal portable (inspired no doubt by Columbia's model 100, 'the Cadet' but not a copy of it) survives and is pictured within this book. It was referred to as the 'sloping' portable as the pictures show. Whether the other prototypes are still in existence is not known at this time.

The main objective for the first half of 1929 was to concentrate on selling existing models. It was proposed to reduce in price the basic black 101 portable from £7 to £6. Various figures for factory output were discussed, as reduced prices of the portable might increase demand and affect the manufacture of other models including the proposed ones! In addition, the demand for equipments (the collective name used for all the parts of machines minus the case) manufactured for foreign factories, especially France, during the previous year had increased. Foreign factories included those in Germany, Spain, Czechoslovakia, France, and India. The company hoped that new models would only be put on the market when the stocks of existing models were exhausted. The

THE PERFECT GRAMOPHONE
FOR THE OPEN AIR!

New Reduced Prices.

From £6.
(This price does not apply in the Irish Free State.)

On the beach, in the woods, up the river, or wherever you may be, there is no instrument to compare with "His Master's Voice" Portable. It is so light that you carry it with ease, it is so compact that everything you want is inside, and its tone is so good and so full that it gives you real musical satisfaction even when played under the broad vault of the sky. It is the most amazing little portable in the world—"His Master's Voice" tone, "His Master's Voice" design and "His Master's Voice" finish. If you prefer your portable in colour you can get it in Red, Blue, Green or Grey.

"His Master's Voice"
THE FASHIONABLE PORTABLE

The Gramophone Company Ltd., London, W.1.

Printed by Herbert Heather, at the Printing Offices of Messrs. Bradbury, Agnew & Co., Limited, 18-20, Phoenix Place, Mount Pleasant, W.C.1, and published weekly by him in the Office at 30-34, New Bridge Street, in the City of London.—WEDNESDAY, August 7, 1929.

Sitting back to enjoy the outdoors, August 1929.

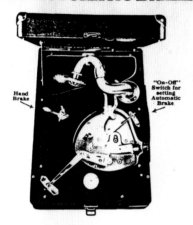

Another Selling Point for Model 102
NEW AUTOMATIC BRAKE

Hand Brake

"On-Off" Switch for setting Automatic Brake

MODEL 102 is packed so full of good selling points that it is difficult to imagine another being added, but this has been done by incorporating a new form of automatic brake. This brake will automatically stop the turntable at the end of all 8-inch, 10-inch, or 12-inch records having a quick run-in groove, whether eccentric as on "His Master's Voice" and "Zonophone" records or spiral as on "Columbia," "Regal," etc.

In addition, a simple "on-off" switch is provided, by means of which the automatic brake can be thrown completely out of action. Control of the turntable is then by means of the simple hand brake which is fitted.

The advantages of this arrangement are obvious, for the ordinary type of automatic brake may present certain difficulties in operation. For example, if it were desired to repeat certain passages in a record the movement of the tone-arm might cause the automatic brake to stop the record; or if one wished to play very small records, or records which run to a centre of very small diameter, the brake might operate before the end of the recording.

In Model 102 these difficulties cannot arise. There is no kind of record, large or small, eccentric or spiral groove, which cannot be played on Model 102. Not only is the repetition of certain passages facilitated, but the playing of novelty records with several grooves, such as puzzle and limerick records, is greatly simplified.

In its original form Model 102 was absolutely unapproached. Here is another selling point which will put it still farther ahead of competition, introduced, too, in ample time for you to make the most of the approaching portable season.

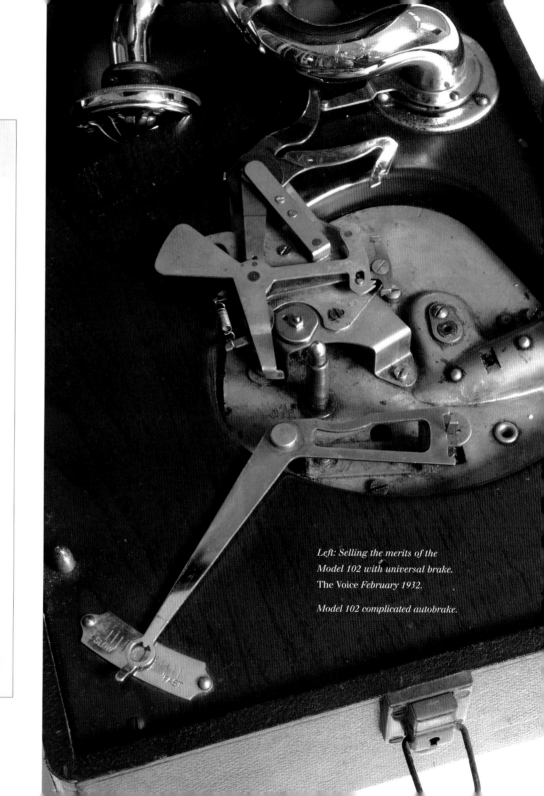

Left: Selling the merits of the Model 102 with universal brake. The Voice *February 1932.*

Model 102 complicated autobrake.

launch date of the new (still unnamed) portable, along with the cheaper version, looked to be autumn 1929. But design problems hindered progress with the two new proposed gramophones throughout 1929 and into 1930. Several meetings took place early in 1931 to try and reconcile the remaining issues holding back manufacturing. At least by this time the 'superior' of the two models had been allocated a catalogue number of 102 and the less expensive model, 99.

A delivery date of 8 April 1931 was set for the model 102 and 65,000 units were earmarked for manufacture – 7,500 for the actual launch. In addition, one hundred each of the 102 and 99 would be needed as advance production models.

In February, there were a couple of issues to confront. First, whether the 'super de-luxe' red leather with gilt fittings version would carry over from the model 101 to the 102. It was considered inconvenient to have one version requiring its own department in the factory but it was decided to continue with it for the time being. However, this and some other coloured versions were later abandoned. Chromium plating had already been introduced on the later model 101s and at that time continued with the portable model 102 only, as there was no room for expansion to other models. Corner shields for the case and a record carrier were also considered. A record carrier replaced the record pocket utilised on the model 101 and sat on the turntable to house 14 ten-inch records.

Initially, it was thought that corner shields on the cases of coloured machines would match the leather-cloth. Eventually, black machines were the only versions to have matching shields; the de-luxe models had none.

Work continued on a new 'universal' brake, designed to stop at the end of any record with a run out groove. It was a very complicated device as the illustrations show. Problems with the design and failure during testing at the factory caused many delays to the planned delivery date of model 102. At almost every weekly meeting, this was put further back, causing frustration and concern that the assembly floor would grind to a halt. Storage of completed machines awaiting the new brake were mounting up. The delays also affected the shipping of 'equipments' to foreign factories, of which 30,000 sets were needed. Contingencies were considered; for example, utilising the automatic brake already used on later model 101s. The motor was pierced for each option.

Below: The famous 'Hear the Bass!' cover.

Right: An orchestra in your home with records was a big selling ploy.

One of several meetings to discuss progress took place on 8 April, the original date for the launch of the model 102. The launch date slipped to June 17, which threatened the production of the planned less expensive model 99.

Tests of the 'universal' brake continued over the coming weeks. All tests were failures. As the end of April approached, with no sign of the the 'universal' brake being successfully developed, attachment of the old brake to 25,000 machines and equipments commenced. As you might have guessed, within a week of taking this action, the 'universal' brake was passing its stringent tests. An order to remove the old brake and replace it with the new one caused more delays. A week before the deadline of June 17 loomed, a new launch date of 15 July was agreed.

No sooner was the 'universal' brake issue resolved (for the time being anyway), the old problem with the no. 5 soundbox reared its ugly head again. His Master's Voice considered their test standards to be more thorough than their old rivals, Columbia. Consequently, only 50% of the new soundboxes passed the stringent tests, but most of the rejects were deemed to be good enough for use on the cheaper model 99.

Another solution was at hand. A new soundbox – the no. 16 – was chosen for use on the first 102s and for all 99s.

Part 5
His Master's Voice
Model 102
(1931-1960)

The Model 102 finally replaced the 101 in July 1931. It had been planned to introduce the new portables when stocks of the older models were exhausted. By the time the Christmas 1931 advertisement appeared showing the model 102 (*opposite*), stocks of 101s would have been running down.

The model 102's new style case with rounded corners was initially available in the colour range of the last 101s. Grey and brown 102s were dropped around mid-1934. By 1937, the 102 in red leather (with gilt fittings) was no longer available. Black, red, blue and green were offered until the end of production. The last red leather-cloth machines were a bright colour with matching felt turntable mat. (The red turntable mat had previously been a darker colour than the case). The original prices of the 102s were the same as the last 101s:

Dimensions	Closed. 16⅝" x 6¼" x 11¼"
Original prices	Black – £5 12s 6d
	Blue, Brown, Green,
	Red, Grey – £6 0s 0d
	Red Leather – £8 8s 0d

Prices were unchanged at the end of 1940.

This Christmas give "THE GOOD COMPANION"

. . . *it carries the* FINEST ENTERTAINMENT *round the house—or round the world*

NO gift can give so much pleasure in so many places as the "His Master's Voice" Portable. It has always been recognised as the one portable gramophone designed, first and foremost, to be a supreme musical instrument. And now there is a new model incorporating many improvements—**without any increase in price.**

Everything is new . . . cabinet, all-metal soundbox, detachable metal tray for 14 records. "Slip-in" winding handle. Automatic brake that works on any record. One-hand lid stay. Chromium plating.

THE NEW

"His Master's Voice" PORTABLE

The fittings were chrome plated. Pre-war coloured machines did not have metal protective corner shields, although black machines had blackened metal shields over the rounded corners. The lid had a new stay, this time on the left of the lid, which remained in place, whether fully opened or not, thanks to a sprung catch. The tone arm was a larger bore than that of the 101. It had a metal fronted soundbox backed with fabric, the no. 16. This was replaced first by the no. 5a, (an improved version of the no. 5 soundbox that had caused so many problems), then the 5b. The one-piece motor board (made of painted metal on early models) incorporated the internal horn, moulded beneath, wrapped around the new motor. The winding handle [37] was a new splined design, which did not

Far left: Why not buy the new Model 102 for your loved one for Christmas? Dec. 1931 supplement.

Below: An original packing carton for the Model 102.

Right: Promoting the Model 102 (record cover illustration).

require screwing into the motor to start winding up of the spring.

The 102 inherited the basic principles of the 101 and some of the fittings – Tungstyle needle tin clip, winding handle clip and socket, manual brake, and speed indicator plate.[36] On early 102s, the manual brake was not fitted only the 'universal' automatic brake which, with a bit of luck, stopped the turntable whether a record had a run out groove or not. This was still in use until spring 1932.

Another automatic brake was used later that was less complicated and could be turned on or off with a lever, without disengaging it from the base of the tone arm. The manual brake, which had returned, could be used when the automatic brake was turned off.

The corner needle drawer is similar to that of the 101. Early coloured versions had chromium needle drawers. Later 102 models had matching coloured 'plastic' drawers.

Top: Model 102 red leather/gilt fittings with handle stowed.

Above: Model 102 closed.

Right: Model 102 open ready for use.

Above: Model 102 red leather/gilt fittings no. 5b soundbox.

Left: Model 102 3rd autobrake.

Usually 102s have an ivorine identification plate[34] showing the model number. Until recently, it was believed that 102 model 'lettering' started at 102C. However, a red 102 was sold at Christies of Kensington, London in December 1999 with a metal label showing '102B'. The versions ran from 102 with no letter, then 102A to H, but the letters used did not include F or G in Britain.

Below: Poster for the portable gramophone. The Voice, May 1932.

Right: Advertising the Model 102.

I MUSTN'T FORGET MY "HIS MASTER'S VOICE" PORTABLE

"His Master's Voice" portable poster. Feature it in your window.

HEAR how well your re "His Mast GRAMOPH

"HIS MASTER'S VOICE" PORTABLE MODEL 99
This new Portable has neither rival nor competitor, for it represents the highest standard of musical reproduction concentrated into the smallest possible compass.

The Vo

VOLUME XVI
No. 5   May. 1932

THE OFFICIAL

Everyone need

His Mas

PORT

The 102s were supplied with the record carrier previously mentioned, which sat on the turntable. The tray had projecting lugs to engage pegs on the motor board and stop it rotating when the machine was being transported. The tray was lined with felt, matching the turntable mat.

Gramophone production stopped during World War II around mid-1941 when only 2,000 102s were assembled to meet expected home sales for the year. (Orders for other models and equipments were also reduced for this period). Some limited stocks were used to replace dealers stocks destroyed in the Blitz.

Above right: Model 102 red open, record tray on turntable.

Below right: Model 102 closed.

Right: Model 102 with record tray out.

Left: Promoting the portable gramophone, The Voice, cover feature, May 1932.

There are many variations found on 102s. I have found on raising the turntable of 102s with no. 16 soundboxes that the motor-boards are cut-away, revealing most of the motor and complicated brake assembly. The motor-board reverts to other more standard drilled hole types later when the 'universal' brake was abandoned. I have also seen machines with 5a soundboxes and cut away motor-boards. 5a machines sometimes have another variation to the Tungstyle clip (the 4th style) as illustrated.[29]

The main differences between the 5a and 5b soundboxes were around the diaphragm and needle bar attachment and the metal cover (the latter was cosmetic). The 5b soundbox is present on several of the 102Cs I have examined and so may have been introduced from that version.

Model 102s were available for export only in 1945 when production re-commenced. From the period 1946 to 1953, there was only a spasmodic availability of machines for the UK market. From January 1946 the 102, now the 102D, was available for the home market in small quantities, whilst the factory toiled to meet commitments for orders abroad. A new launch was set for May 1946 with a limited advertising campaign. Unfortunately, the overseas orders took longer to clear and it wasn't until October 1946 that a few 102s were offered to the trade again and only in black at first, with no tray or pegs.

Front and back of advertising leaflet for Model 102.

ALL THIS FOR £5 . 12 . 6
The Portable model "102" is fitted with the latest type soundbox, giving an exceptionally wide range of musical frequencies. The case, in black waterproof leather cloth, is of modern design with rounded corners. All metal parts are chromium plated. The winding key is of the slip-in type with a long inclined crank for easy winding, and the automatic stop works without setting. The lid stay can be operated with one hand; and the detachable metal tray on the turn-table carries fourteen 10" records easily and safely.

PRICES: The Portable is also made in:
Red, Green, Blue, Grey and Brown £6 . 0 . 0
Red Leather (gold-plated fittings)   £8 . 8 . 0
       or by convenient Hire Purchase terms.

"LET YOURSELF GO"-ANYWHERE

WITH A

"HIS MASTER'S VOICE"

P O R T A B L E

GET THE PARTY **going** WITH A SWING!

● Just lift the lid, choose your record — you can carry fourteen with you on the detachable metal tray and set everyone's shoulders swaying and fingers snapping to the latest hit played by Ray Noble; set them all dreaming at the bidding of Kreisler the magician; have Stokowski and the 'Philadelphia' crash out the tremendous chords of the '1812' Overture; or Caruso himself sing 'Vesti la Giubba'. All this in the open air — or indoors — on any occasion — from an instrument no larger than an ordinary-sized attaché case, yet with a tone absolutely 'true-to-life'!

SINGING

DANCING

HOT JAZZ

● ANYTIME'S PORTABLE TIME
At the PICNIC
At the PARTY
On the RIVER
In CAMP
On HIKES
At SEA
In the GARDEN
On the LOUNGE

OPERA   ORCHESTRAL   VARIETY   VIOLIN   PIANO

Dealers were warned that shortages of materials meant that some fittings might be different in colour.

In April 1947, the 102 was increased in price to £10 10s – the result of an increase in cost of raw materials and wages. The following year, a standardisation of portable gramophones was proposed, to keep costs down. This meant that all models would be manufactured in essentially the same way. In June 1948, the Company examined how this policy would work. In order to make all models in this way, corner shields would be introduced for the coloured 102s for the first time. This saved effort in manufacture, since the leather cloth was difficult to cut and glue on the rounded corners of the case. This had never been a problem with the black model as it already had blackened metal shields.

It was hoped that the 102 would be available in blue, red and green as well as the standard black. However, big savings were not possible in the manufacture of 102s, as chromium plating for shields and screws for the coloured machines added to costs. The ends of the carrying handle on coloured 102s required plating, as had the pre-war coloured 101 models. Rubber feet were to be incorporated into the bottom case shields, which was another change. Usually, rubber studs were inserted into drilled holes in the case. These may be missing today due to the studs shrinking and dropping out. Larger savings had to be found in the manufacture of other models.

Above: Model 102 grey leatherette with record tray and handle in stowed position.

Right: Model 102 open for use.

Far left: Model 102 with no. 16 soundbox.

Left: Model 102 closed.

Above: Model 102 green closed.

Top: Model 102 open. Handle stowed in the lid.

Right: Model 102 open ready for use.

The His Master's Voice trademark attached to a 'plaque' on the inside of the 102s lid is not present from 102E. (The parts list for the 102D suggested this had already occurred. As both listings were issued at the same time, I suspect this was an error in the cover drawing.) The trademark was placed simply on the inside of the lid. Black machines no longer had polished motor boards, just black leather-cloth. Coloured 102s finally re-emerged in late October 1948.

The trademark transfer and legend 'Made in Gt. Britain' with a brighter green background can be found on some 102Ds and on later versions.

Versions 102D and 102E were both available in September 1950 and had a couple of changes. The flush motor-board was introduced on the 102E, leaving no need for an escutcheon[35]. This development made the 102 easier to produce. The case was adjusted so that the lid was deeper in proportion to allow a shallower base. The Tungstyle needle clip was abandoned.

Export sales of the 102 were dominant – some 31,000 during 1950, compared with a home sales figure of around 11,000. Low home sales were due to the Company's export demand and shortages of wood and steel. 102Es only were available from summer 1951, when shortages of spring steel caused changes to the motors of the portables range and 'a/T' was added to each model number for a short period. It is not certain what this meant, but may have been added to identify machines with shorter springs.

Further cost savings were examined in 1951 when it was suggested that a moulded handle might be substituted for the usual carved and painted wooden grip.

It appears that from around 1951, for two and a half years, manufacturing of 102s was all for export, the model appearing again as the 102H in mid-March 1953 in limited numbers, in black only at £11 2s 11d. Blue, red and green models returned later when export demands had been satisfied.

Catalogues showed the 102 available up to 30 June 1960 being assembled from left over parts for the previous two or three years.

Top: Model 102 blue closed.

Above: Model 102 with ivorine plate and speed control.

Left: No. 5b soundbox and arm.

Right: Model 102 blue ready for use.

69

Model	His Master's Voice 102
Production date	Late July 1931-1960.
	By 1960 sales would be from stock.
Colours	As 101G (early) until 1934 when grey and brown versions were abandoned. Only black, blue, green, and red leather-cloth available from 1937. Indian 102s were painted in various colours and designs in the 1930s, including a banding effect. (See Tropical Models section).
Soundbox	No. 16, 5a (102 A-Bs) 5b (102C onwards).
Motors used:	102–271C (until at least October 1931).
Versions identified	102A-C, 271D, 102D, 102DX, 102E, 270D.
	A Columbia version of the 102 was available called the model 9000, with soundbox no. 28 – actually a copy of the His Master's Voice no.5b! Not all of the characteristics of the 102 were adopted at first due to existing contractual agreements between Columbia and Garrard in the 1930s. Columbia models 9000 and 9000A also used motor 270D.
Escutcheon	Style 7 (until model 102E when escutcheons were no longer present due to lack of space).
Catch/lock	Similar to Style 7[55] New, single-action type on D-H.
Fittings	Chromium plated (later needle drawers in matching 'plastic' on coloured machines, blackened metal on black machines).
Identifying plate	Third style ivorine or metal on early machines. Fourth style ivorine from 102C.
Winding handle	Style 4[57]
Carrying handle	Usually as 101D (Pakawa) with some variations during World War II.
Notes for collectors	Black machines had wood-grained or wood motor-boards until 102H. After 102E, lids on the case were deeper; all black version motor-boards were covered in black leather-cloth; coloured machines had chromium corner shields. Carrying handles varied especially during the 1940s, which may have been due to wartime shortages. Model 102 instruction cards ceased having a picture on the cover from around version 102C.

Model 102 brown.

"HIS MASTER'S VOICE"
Portable Gramophone

MODEL 102H

Reproducing all types of music and speech with equal clarity and "true-to-life" tone, this H.M.V. instrument is in the very forefront of portable gramophone design. Extremely handsome in appearance, light in weight and robust in construction, it will give lasting pleasure on any occasion, indoors or out. Model 102H is built specifically to withstand the rigours of travelling, all movable components being held rigidly in position in transit.

Please see over for further details.

"HIS MASTER'S VOICE"

The Hallmark of Quality

*Above: Model 102 green
(with banding) tropical open
and closed.*

*Left: The final version of
the Model 102 (Model 102H)
from leaflet c1958.*

Accessories for the portable models 101 and 102s

His Master's Voice offered accessories to upgrade an acoustic soundbox to an electrical one (see illustrations). As both advertisements feature portable models 101 and 102, the Gramophone Company must have appreciated the importance of the portable in the home. An electric pick-up would certainly restrict the use of the portable machine outdoors at the time though.

Needle container, speed tester, soundbox container, .

Some other accessories

Of course, these were in addition to the various other 'indispensable' items offered for sale for the gramophone owner. Included were record dusters, fibre needle cutters, speed testers, record albums, and other items now in great demand by 'Nipper' collectors. Even tubes of authentic His Master's Voice grease and bottles of oil are eagerly sought. With original boxes and instruction leaflets their value increases substantially.

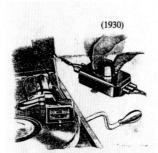

(1930)

A Pick-up for any Gramophone

Fixes direct to tone arm, replacing existing soundbox and instantly converts gramophone to a playing desk for electrical reproduction. Complete with volume control and shielded leads. Adjustable to any radio receiver.

No. 11 Pick-up Attachment

£2 : 2 : 0

(1933)

Make YOUR Gramophone a RADIOGRAM—and double the joys of your wireless set

BY means of this pick-up—the same as that used on "His Master's Voice" Radiograms—any acoustic gramophone can be instantly converted into a radio-gramophone in conjunction with a radio set. The pick-up can be attached at once, without any adjustment, to your tone-arm in place of your existing soundbox, and is supplied complete with screened leads and a logarithmic volume control. In the volume control, provision is made for matching the impedance of the pick-up to any type of receiver.

(Pick-up Model 11)

Electric Pick-up No.11
Fitted to a 101 (left) and to a 102 (right). The pick-up was supplied with an adaptor which allowed its use with a narrow or medium bore tone arm.

Above: Advertisements for electric pickup no. 11 from 1930 and 1933.

Right: Covers promoting electric pickup no. 11, tungstyle needles and accessories.

Far right: Model 102 advertisement, c1957.

"His Master's Voice"

PORTABLE GRAMOPHONES...

- **The Gramophone** you have always wanted — handsome, lightweight, robust, ready to go anywhere!

- **Large** sound aperture and acoustically correct soundbox ensure lifelike reproduction and maximum volume.

- **Powerful** spring motor plays even 12" 78 r.p.m records at *one winding*, runs silently, lasts for years!

- **Calibrated** speed regulator ensures correct reproduction, while the gramophone has both automatic stop *and* hand brake.

- **Gleaming** chromium plating protects metal fittings.

- **Husky** hardwood cabinet, weatherproof leathercloth covering in BLACK, GREEN, BLUE or RED, leather carrying handle and metal corner-pieces combine handsome appearance with rugged durability. Take your Model 102 portable gramophone everywhere — at home, in the garden, on holiday — for perfect, portable pleasure.

DIMENSIONS (approx.) 6″ x 11½″ x 16½″ (15.2 x 29.2 x 41.9 cm.)

WEIGHT 16 lbs. (7.3 ks.)

Needle tins once perhaps given with the purchase of a secondhand gramophone, and dusters, have found another group of dedicated collectors and rare examples can attract high prices. They come in various styles, sizes and makes and are, without doubt, a hobby by themselves.

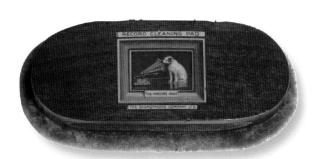
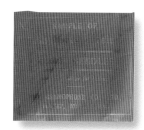

Part 6
His Master's Voice
Model 99
(1931-1933)

As already discussed, the Gramophone Company had been looking to introduce two new portables to take over from the 101. Whilst there had been several delays over the design and testing of parts for the 102, plans for the new, less expensive model, the 99, was also ongoing. The difficulties with the 102's new 'universal' brake gave rise to concern that the launch of the 99 would be delayed too. The 99 was to be launched later than the 102 and the tools required to make certain parts for it were due to be ready by the end of July 1931.

It had already been decided to use the old type automatic brake that had been fitted to later 101s. Weekly meetings provided updates on the progress of the model. It was hoped that production would start on time and that the delivery date would be 9 September. A manufacturing order for 100,000 machines was made. The 99 would not have a record pocket like the 101 nor a record carrier. This time an album would be used for housing records in the lid. In a meeting on 28 April, three colours were proposed for the model, black, blue, and red. The motor board, which would be made from metal, was to be painted. The same finish was also requested for lining the cabinet, but this was later rescinded. It was decided that record

Model 99 red open.
Record holder stowed
in lid, winding handle
in case.

albums would be bought from outside suppliers in the appropriate colours. Equipments of model 99s for foreign factories would not include the album, which would have to be purchased locally.

By 23 June, the model 99 was in production to meet the September delivery date.

Dimensions	15" x 11½" x 5¼"
Original prices	Black – £3 5s 0d
	Red or Blue – £3 10s 0d
Turntable size	8¾". (Some turntables were made of light alloy rather than steel).

Right: Model 99 open.
Record folder outside,
handle ready to play.

Below: Model 99 closed.

77

As on the 102, the internal horn was moulded beneath the motor board as one piece. The motor had a single horizontal spring, which, in line with the overall design of the machine, was smaller than the other portables discussed so far.

The motor board was made from painted steel, brown for the black version to simulate wood, and red or blue on the others. The fittings were either screwed into the metal (speed control, auto-brake, tone arm) or riveted (speed indicator plate[38] winding handle clip[39]).

Polyfar (German) record cover.

The auto-brake worked from a pawl and boss activated by the eccentric cut off groove on most 78s of the time. The brake was a little harsh, but effective. Lifting the tone arm off the record and to the right released the brake. Returning the tone arm to its support, allowed the turntable to run less than a quarter turn before the brake re-engaged.

Unlike the 100, 101 and 102, where piano hinges and stay were used for the lid, the 99 hinges held the lid in place by supporting oblong rings (there was no lid stay.) This meant that the lid tended to lean backwards.

Some 99s had 'ring-less' hinges, appearing to have been 'tapped' rather than screwed into the case. As the horn wound anti-clockwise, the mouth of the horn emerged from the right of the machine. For these reasons, the lid did not direct the sound as on the other portables. What it lacked in tone was certainly made up for in volume!

The Tungstyle needle clip was positioned on the inside of the lid. There were two small fittings and a spring clip to house the new record album, (as on Decca and Columbia models.)

In many ways, the machine was a mixture of new and old styles. It reverted to the awkward front wind system so that it was impossible to be wound on any flat surface. The tone arm was in one piece, unique for any British His Master's Voice machine. This made changing needles difficult. Unlike the other portables mentioned, the arm did not rotate on ball bearings. Two screws in the 'ball' of the arm

Right: Model 99 blue open.
Below: Model 99 closed.

stabilised the arm in its socket in a thin groove.

The small turntable did not have a raised rim, but appeared in later models – certainly, in the coloured examples I have seen. The felt was the usual brown on the black machine and red or blue on the coloured machines. The protective corner shields[40] are believed to be peculiar to any model in this country, with rubber feet incorporated into the bottom shields. I have seen an illustration of a German portable machine with similar corners.

Being a low cost machine, you might expect the 99 to be more commonly found nowadays, but it's production run was short-lived. The cheaper end of the market had gone to the more successful Columbia models after the formation of EMI. Model 99s when they appear, are often in poor condition, with problems caused by adaptations that have been made. The original tone arm socket was made from a thin, fragile casting, which could be severely damaged with careless handling.

As with budget models from other makers, hardwearing leather-cloth was not used on all the interior surfaces of the machine. The inside of the lid was covered by coloured paper. The black machine had brown paper, the red and blue, a similar colour to the case. This is useful to know, as dampening of this paper in an attempt to clean the machine will cause irreparable damage.

As expected, the black version turns up more often than the two coloured versions. The blue is quite uncommon; the red is rarely seen.

THE "BABY" PORTABLE

This model offers remarkable value for those who require a portable gramophone at an exceptionally low price. It represents the famous "His Master's Voice" standard of reproduction concentrated into the smallest possible compass. Never before has it cost so little to take an instrument round the house or round the world, which will reproduce your favourite records with pleasing tone and good volume. Its features include a new all-metal soundbox No. 16; one-piece tonearm; slip-in winding handle; automatic brake and an album to hold six 10-inch records which can be removed from the lid while the instrument is playing. Specially designed hinges enabling the lid to be raised or lowered with one hand. The wooden cabinet is strongly made and covered in leather cloth, with metal corners.

Model 99

Black	£3 5	0
Red or Blue ..	£3 10	0

Model	His Master's Voice 99
Production date	Late 1931-1933
Colours	Black, red or blue leather-cloth
Soundbox	No. 16
Motors	23b
Escutcheon	Style 1
Catch/lock	No lock. Simple catches x 2. Style 8[41]
Fittings	Blackened inside on black version. Red & blue painted or nickelled outside on the other versions.
Identifying plate	Style 3
Winding handle	Style 5[42]
Carrying handle	Style 2 (Pakawa)

As you can see from the illustrations, the model 99 speed indicator plate differs from those usually found on the models 101 and 102.

In addition, the smaller trademark found on the later 101s and the 102s appeared on the model 99. In my experience, the trademark as shown, is not usually on the 99 record albums held in the lid, although the illustrations (on some record covers) give this impression. The record albums, which housed up to six ten-inch records usually have a trademark in outline, coloured gold. The album, when in place, obscures the trademark in the lid. It doesn't matter too much, as this item is usually missing from the machine. I have owned four model 99s, (two black, one blue and a red). Fortunately, the red machine has the record album. In its restored state, it is a very attractive machine.

His Master's Voice got it right by sometimes referring to the model 99 as 'the junior or baby portable'. However, the 99 was a very low-grade gramophone and never again did His Master's Voice issue anything so cheap and of such poor quality for the home market.

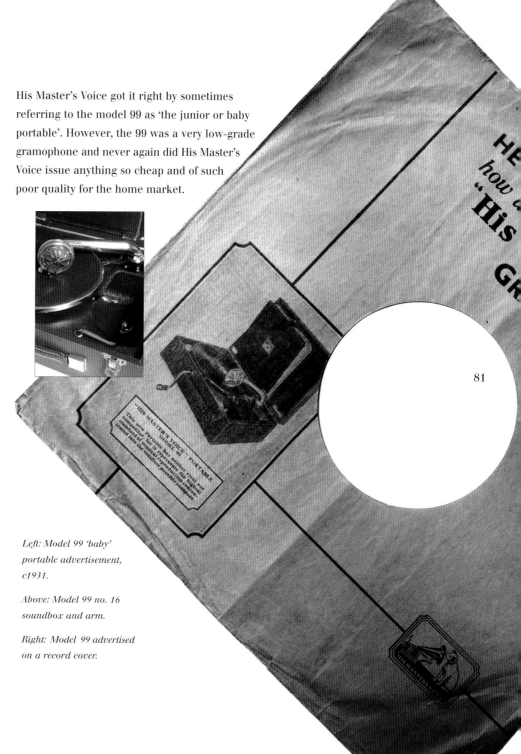

Left: Model 99 'baby' portable advertisement, c1931.

Above: Model 99 no. 16 soundbox and arm.

Right: Model 99 advertised on a record cover.

Part 7
The merger of two giants
(1931)

The effect of the 1929 Wall Street crash heralded the start of the Depression. Like almost every other business, the recording industry was hit hard. In an attempt to attract more business, gramophone and record prices were slashed. An advertisement in *Punch* magazine dated 17 April 1929 announced a reduction of £1 for a standard black model 101 and 10 shillings each for the deluxe models.

The *London Pictorial* in its issue dated 28 April 1929, reported meetings taking place between rivals Columbia and His Master's Voice. *'It is understood that negotiations have been in progress in London for the consolidation of the Columbia Gramophone Company and the HMV (sic) Company. A meeting to arrange terms will probably be held in Paris next week.'*

Clearly the talks dragged on, because in the *News of the World's* finance column of 16 June 1929, it was reported: *'The Gramophone (HMV) Company whose £1 shares are standing in the market at £17 12s 6d each, has announced that shareholders will be offered one new share for every share held at the price of 20s per share. The rights to acquire the new shares are included in the existing price for the old. This means that for £18 12s 6d, plus, of course, commission and stamps, a buyer will secure two Gramophone Company shares.*

There must be a period of some uncertainty for the investor during the next few months – doubt as regards the future, renders the shares of the Gramophone Company rather a doubtful proposition at the moment for the average investor.'

In the spring of 1931 as already discussed, Columbia merged with the Gramophone Company to form Electric and Musical Industries (EMI).

His Master's Voice shopfront advertisement.

*Above: 17 April 1929
advertisement announcing
price reductions.*

*Right: Record supplement
announcing new records
by Sergei Rachmaninoff
and Fritz Kreisler,
March 1931.*

Part 8
His Master's Voice
EMI Portables and
the end of an era
(1934-1960)

His Master's Voice Model 97 (1934-60)

The models His Master's Voice 97 and Columbia
204 were the first portables to emerge from the
newly formed EMI. With the formation of EMI in
June 1931, it was possible to 'borrow' certain items
from what had been the opposition's models. For
example, the soundbox used was the Columbia 15a
with Nipper's likeness on the front on His Master's
Voice versions. Surprisingly, the two versions used
slightly different motors, the 97 motor no. 220B,
and the 204 motor 220D. (It should be noted that
Columbia had had a long running contract with
Garrard to provide motors for their gramophones).

The His Master's Voice branding was just
badge engineering, both machines with 'the Dog'
or with the Columbia 'Magic Notes' trademarks
had little else to differentiate them. Nowadays,
there is more demand for a gramophone with
Nipper's likeness than most other makes. People
just seem to have a great affection for him.

The model 97 was like a 'budget version' of
the model 102, which as previously discussed was
still in production. His Master's Voice (and the
Columbia version, model 204) were described as
an 'inexpensive portable'. Like the 102, the 97 had

*Above: Model 97 open,
record tray on turntable.*

Above left: Model 97 closed.

*Left: Model 97 open,
tray off turntable.*

Left: Advertisement for the Model 97.

Below: Model 97 autobrake and ivorine plate.

Bottom: A dealer using a record cover to sell His Master's Voice gramophones.

85

a record storage tray on pre-war versions, although it managed without the two pegs of early model 102s. So, the tray did not need or have lugs. The His Master's Voice 97 was available in Britain from 1934 until around 1940. Each version is identifiable by an ivorine plate (as with 102s). The black version was available first, followed by coloured versions around January 1937. (Post-war, the Columbia version only was sold in Britain. The model 204a made way for model 204b, the same machine but with chromium plated instead of nickel parts).

Dimensions	Closed. 15" x 11½" x 5⅞".
Original prices	Black – £3 10s 0d
	Red, Blue or Green – £3 15s 0d

By November 1940 the 97 was priced at £3 15s for any colour. The motor board on the model 97 was one piece, covered in the appropriate colour of leatherette (black, blue, red or green). Like the models 101 and 102, the case was fitted with the corner needle drawer, positioned lower down the case than the usual halfway point. Metal studs replaced protective metal shields. The speed indicator plate[44] was a variation to that provided on the model 99. Above the letters 's' for slow and 'f' for fast were two raised prongs that acted as stops for the speed pointer. The escutcheon[45] was quite small. The winding handle[43] was another variation of the 'slip in' variety, using the cruder

Models 102 and 97 from the 1936 catalogue.

MODEL 102

THE FINEST PORTABLE OBTAINABLE

THE audibly superior tone of this "His Master's Voice" Portable Model is due to two factors, possessed by the "His Master's Voice" Portable alone. A No. 5a sound-box, and the design of the horn which is of exceptional length.

It is an instrument with everything to commend it. Every detail is as perfect as past experience and present knowledge can make it.

It is full of neat contrivances. The handle is instantly detachable from its resting-place and is so designed that you can wind the gramophone up when it is standing on a table, without barking your knuckles. A special tray on the turntable carries twelve 10-inch records inside with complete safety. An automatic brake, speed control, and handbrake are also fitted. In black waterproof cloth **£5 12s. 6d.** In colours, Red, Green or Blue, **£6 0s. 0d.** Or by Hire Purchase.

"HIS MASTER'S VOICE"

MODEL 97

INEXPENSIVE PORTABLE

THIS model is similar in many respects to Model 102. It incorporates some of the refinements of the larger instrument, including a carrying tray to take twelve 10-inch records, automatic brake, speed control, hand-brake and built-in needle cup.

Reproduction is of " His Master's Voice " standard, but has not quite the same power and frequency range as the more expensive instrument. The single spring motor plays ten or twelve inch records at a single winding, and the winding key is of the quick engagement type. The case is finished in waterproofed cloth, and is exceptionally light to carry.

Price : In black, **£3 10s. 0d.** In colours, Red, Blue or Green, **£3 15s. 0d.** Or by Hire Purchase.

"HIS MASTER'S VOICE"

method of a slot in the end of the winding shaft to locate in the motor. This was a hark back to much earlier machines, as was the small catch or lock which seemed based on an early model 101 style. The lid stay, positioned on the left hand side of the lid, disappears into a small well when closed.

Model	His Master's Voice 97
Production date	1934 to late 1950s.
Colours	Black, red, blue or green leather-cloth.
Soundbox	No.21 (disguised Columbia 15a).
Motors	Details are provided only for completeness. There are differences in motors even when spring barrels are identical.
	97 (no lettering) No. 220B
	Version A No. 748B
	Version B No. 794C
	Version C No. 26590F
	Version C (later) No. 26590E (with silent brake)
	Columbia version
	Model 204 No. 220D
	Model 204B No. 794D
	Model 204C No. 26590D
	Model 204C (later) No. 26590F
Fittings	Chromium (with coloured plastic or blackened metal needle corner drawer).
Identifying plate	Style 4 Ivorine.
Carrying handle	Pakawa.

Model 97 no. 21 soundbox and arm.

88

Model 97 came in versions A to E. The instruction card (in chapter 9) is for version B. Both 97A and Bs were available in November 1935 and the parts lists for the 97 shows the differences between the two, mainly motor related. The author has seen model 97s with ivorine plates clearly marked B3 (ie 1939) with model no. 97 and model 97C shown.

A typical advertisement for Model 97.

"His Master's Voice" Portable
Number Ninety-Seven

SPECIFICATION

Sturdily built, beautiful finish.
Strong Cabinet, covered in black fabric: "Pakawa" handle.
Size: 15 ins. x 11½ ins. x 5¾ ins.
Single spring motor to play 10-inch and 12-inch records, with auto stop.
New style quick engagement winding key.
Record carrier, fitting on turntable to carry 12 10-inch records.
Closed edge pattern turntable covered in felt.
New taper, with crook tone arm, combined with horn of special construction and musically perfect sound box.
Needle box in corner of cabinet.
All internal fittings nickel-plated, all external fittings black.

PRICE
£3 : 10 : 0
or by hire purchase

Model: His Master's Voice 87 (circa 1937-41)

In addition to the other portables featured in this book was the model 87, which was for export only. It had a long spindle for the storage of records and may have started out with a straight tone arm. It is possible that later versions reverted to a standard Columbia tone arm. Otherwise, it was pretty much like the model 97. (For information only, the motors nos. 794B and 27040C were used on this model). The version 87A used motor no. 26590B. (The Columbia version was model 205 which used motor 794B).

*Model 87 shown
here minus soundbox.*

*Right: Model 87
instruction leaflet.*

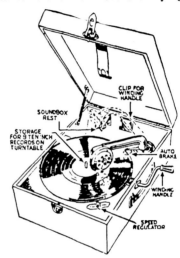

"HIS MASTER'S VOICE"
PORTABLE GRAMOPHONE
MODEL 87.

(With Automatic brake and record-carrying turntable.)

SOUNDBOX REST

CLIP FOR WINDING HANDLE

STORAGE FOR 9 TEN INCH RECORDS ON TURNTABLE

AUTO BRAKE

WINDING HANDLE

SPEED REGULATOR

HOW TO SET UP THE INSTRUMENT (see Illustration)

(Please read these instructions right through before attempting to operate the instrument

The Portable having been unpacked and opened (the key is tied to the handle, proceed as follows :—

Pull out the winding handle which will be found clipped to the side of the well and slip it straight into the winding sleeve just above the carrying handle. Wind the motor up fully by turning the winding handle in a clockwise direction and place a record on the turntable. Now turn the soundbox crook arm back and insert an "His Master's Voice" needle in the soundbox. Screw up the needle screw firmly.

A sample packet of "His Master's Voice" needles is included in the equipment of this Portable.

TO START TURNTABLE

Hold the soundbox in the right hand and swing the tone arm over to the right. This will release the automatic brake, thus allowing the turntable to revolve. Lower the needle gently on to the smooth edge of the record and slide into the first groove.

The automatic brake will automatically stop records which have an eccentric or a quick run-in finishing groove.

Speed of Turntable.

All records should be played at the speed marked on the record label. "His Master's Voice" records are all made at a uniform speed of 78 revolutions per minute, therefore records should be played at that speed. Adjust speed by means of the speed regulator.

Model: His Master's Voice 88 (circa 1941-60)

This model replaced model 87 around 1941, as a 'really cheap' priced portable for the export market. EMI felt there was a need to provide a machine that would fill the gap in the market for those customers abroad who wanted a cheap gramophone.

The motor used on this model was no. 26590E. Presumably, manufacturing started shortly after this date with a Columbia version available (model 211 a redesign of the model 204). By the summer of 1951, as discussed earlier, the temporary range of all portable gramophones with the prefix '/T' model 88s (still model 88A) was available in black, blue, and green. Large numbers of this model were still available for export in 1960. An Irish catalogue dated 1955 proves that the model 88 was offered in that country, but not in Britain.

Records at EMI confirm that two other variations of motors were also in use on later EMI portable gramophones, 26590G and 26590H. Further details are not known.

Model 88, blue leatherette version.

THE VOICE

VOLUME XII   No. 6   JUNE, 1928

A MONTHLY REVIEW PUBLISHED
BY THE GRAMOPHONE COMPANY,
LIMITED, 363-367, OXFORD STREET,
LONDON, W.I.

IN THE INTEREST OF BETTER AND
GREATER BUSINESS FOR THEIR
DEALERS AND THEMSELVES

92

Clearing stock

His Master's Voice finally stopped making goods and closed the factory between 1957/8. By the end of the 1950s, the days of the portable acoustic clockwork gramophones were nearly over. It would seem that EMI had quite a large amount of stock to dispose of. With some 36,000 finished machines, it was uncertain as to how they were going to sell all of them. The Company turned its attention to exporting them to African colonies, with incentive schemes based on advertising allowances and turnover. Eyes also turned to Ceylon, Iceland and Singapore. The main concern was the high stock levels of model 102s, (around 24,000), and model 88s of which there were 12,000. Apart from complete machines, there was a large quantity of 'equipments' to clear, which included everything but cases. Some of these were destined for India, where they were assembled in locally made cases.

And so, the clockwork gramophone slid into history. 78s are still in abundance if you know where to look. There are rarities worth a lot of money but most popular 78s are not worth much more than 50p. Prices of some gramophone models are upwardly mobile but portables are still within the reach of most collectors.

I hope this book has encouraged you to start reappraising the humble portable with the dog trademark and to consider starting a collection.

The Voice, promoting portable gramophones, June 1928.

Part 9
His Master's Voice
Portable Gramophone
Instruction Cards

Instruction cards (or leaflets) accompanied most
new His Master's Voice gramophones including
the range of portable models. (I have not yet seen
a card for the model 100). Basic information on
setting up the machine and how to lubricate the
clockwork motor was provided. With the arrival of
the model 101, a label was glued to the bottom of
the case showing where to use grease or oil the
gramophone motor to maintain performance.
The purchaser was also encouraged to buy and
use generic accessories and needles.

I have included a list of instruction cards as
they rarely turn up now with gramophones. The
original owners presumably discarded them soon
after purchase. I have some originals but manage
with copies of others, as do other collectors. I
would certainly welcome further information or
cards to add to the list.

For reference a table of known instruction
cards appear on page 94.

Four Model 101
instruction cards.

93

Model & ref. letter	Issue ref.	Part no.
101C		9206C
101E		9206D
101G		9206G
101L		9206E
102	No ref. but shows universal auto brake	Not shown
102	A/Issue 1	8776
102	A/Issue 4	8776
102	A/Issue 5	8776
102	A/Issue 6	8776
102	A/Issue 7	8776
102	Issue 4*	8776
99		994
97	Issue 1B	21351
97	Issue 2(D)**	33463
87	Issue 2	12646

* Issue 4 came later than the A/ series and shows an illustration of the then current version of the gramophone with 'flush' motor board.

** Issue 2(D) refers to a known card supplied with Australian and other export model 97s.

Four Model 102 instruction cards.

"HIS MASTER'S VOICE"
Portable Gramophone
MODEL 99

Instructions for Assembling and Operating

Part No. 994

HOW TO ASSEMBLE AND OPERATE

His Master's Voice
PORTABLE GRAMOPHONE
MODEL 97

THIS CARD MUST BE DELIVERED WITH THE INSTRUMENT TO THE USER

Part No. 21354

Issue 1B

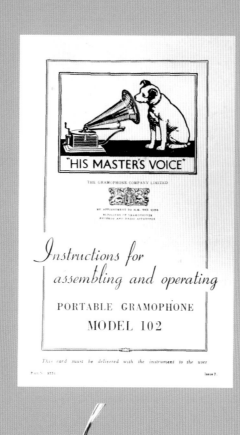

THE GRAMOPHONE COMPANY LIMITED

BY APPOINTMENT TO H.M. THE KING
SUPPLIERS OF GRAMOPHONE
RECORDS AND RADIO APPARATUS

*Instructions for
assembling and operating*

PORTABLE GRAMOPHONE
MODEL 102

This card must be delivered with the instrument to the user

Part No. 8776

Issue 7.

See that this hand Brake is in the "off" position (lever towards turn-table), and that "Auto-Brake" lever is set to "on" before attempting to use auto-brake.

Issue 1.

Part No. 16428

INSTRUCTIONS
for
assembling and operating
H.M.V. MODEL 102
PORTABLE GRAMOPHONE

"HIS MASTER'S VOICE"

The Hallmark of Quality

PART No. 8776
ISSUE 4

THIS CARD MUST BE DELIVERED WITH THE INSTRUMENT TO THE USER

*Model 102
instruction cards.*

95

"HIS MASTER'S VOICE"

E 615 H·M·V ENGLISH

Part 10
Tropical Models
(1928-1957)

In addition to the teak version of models 100 and 101 for the Indian market, there were also other tropical models to choose from.

His Master's Voice Model 112 (1928-1933)
The Camp Portable (first version)
The 112 was really a model 101 with the number 32 vertical double spring motor instead of one of the new-style horizontal single-spring motors. The teak case was much deeper than the 101, to house the larger motor. As such, it was not an ideal portable machine, resembling a standard table gramophone in both size and weight. Unlike most table machines, it could only be played with the lid open but it had a carrying handle! Built in India, the Gramophone Company realised that it was 'very heavy' and only considered portable in that country and unsuitable to European conditions. This machine appears to have been available abroad between 1928 and 1933, and an example in the Royal Scottish Museum is datable to that period. It is made of teak and has the recently introduced circular gold transfer identifying the model number. The gold transfer is rather badly placed, next to the brake lever and with regular use can be worn away. The machine comes with either gilt or nickel-plated fittings. The protective metal shields are present.

Indian art deco cover.

The lid resembled the 'tropical' 101, but as with other tropical machines, had no ferrule in the record pocket. In all other respects, it appears similar to a teak 101.

His Master's Voice Model 113 (Circa. 1931-1941)
The Transportable
In many ways this model is the king sized portable. It is easily large and heavy enough to be classed as a table model gramophone, the difference being that it has a carrying handle. Features include a double-spring motor (no. 32M), 12-inch turntable, 5a or 5b soundbox, automatic brake and nickel-plated shields and parts (chrome for the last year 1940-1941). There are two main differences between this tropical model and the 'camp' model. The 'flap door' which pulls down at the front to reveal the grill over the mouth of the horn and of course the horn itself. This is the only portable machine to have a full size table model horn. This version of the horn produces wonderful sound quality. As with all tropical models, the 113 is quite uncommon in Britain. They only appear if the owner brought one home.

His Master's Voice Model 114 (Circa. 1934-1941)
The Camp Portable (second version)
This model was an updated Camp portable based on the 102 with a double spring motor (no. 32). Many of the comments made about the model 112 and its relationship to the 101 apply to the 114.

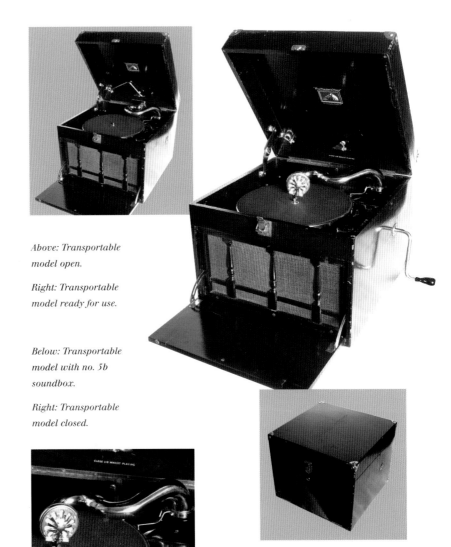

Above: Transportable model open.

Right: Transportable model ready for use.

Below: Transportable model with no. 5b soundbox.

Right: Transportable model closed.

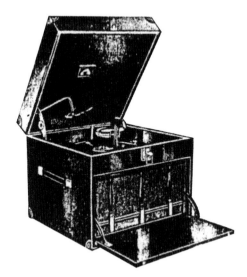

Model 113
transportable model.

Below: Model 114 open and
closed.

The 114 was available in brown leather-cloth or highly polished teak. It had chromium-plated parts including corner shields, 10-inch turntable, auto-brake and no. 5a soundbox. (The 114c had the no. 5b soundbox). The 114 was only available for a short time and not after 1941. At present there is limited information available on the following Indian models. There are no Indian catalogues held in EMI archives for the period 1928 and 1929 or between 1942 and 1955.

His Master's Voice Tropical Models – Dimensions, prices & finishes

Model	Dimensions (machine closed)	Original price (rupees)	Finishes
Model 102	16¼" x 5⅞" x 11⅜"	105	Black leatherette
		115	Highly polished cabinet (mahogany finish with black embossed lines)
		115	Blue, green, red leatherette
Model 112	17½" x 12½" x 9"	155	Oak finished cabinet or brown leatherette
Model 113	13⁹⁄₁₆" x 16¹¹⁄₁₆" x 16⁷⁄₁₆"	180 (1940 - 185)	Highly polished cabinet
Model 114	9¼" x 12⁵⁄₁₆" x 17¹⁵⁄₁₆"	145 (1940 - 140)	Highly polished cabinet (with black embossed lines)
		140 (1940 - 135)	Brown leatherette
Model 94	15" x 11½" x 6¾"	100	Highly polished cabinet
		90	Brown leatherette
Model 118	17¼" x 12¼" x 9¾"	145	Highly polished cabinet (with black embossed lines)
Model 300	15¾" x 11¼" x 6¾"	145	Black
		152	Blue, green, red leatherette
Model 301	16¾" x 14¾" x 17"	395	Highly polished veneered cabinet
Model 302	15½" x 11" x 6¼"	105	Black
Model 303	15¾" x 11¼" x 6¾"	152½	Black
		157½	Blue, green, red leatherette

His Master's Voice Model 94 *(c.1939)*

This machine, for export only, which was available with canvas cover and was supplied with record carrier and no. 21 soundbox, may have been short lived. The motor used was the 27040B.

His Master's Voice Model 118 *(c.1936-1941)*

This model was unusual in that the case opened lengthways. It had a 10-inch turntable, double spring motor, auto-brake and no. 5B soundbox.

His Master's Voice De-luxe Model 300 *(c.1956)*

This was a deluxe portable model on the lines of
the model 102, available in black, red, green, and
blue with a double spring motor. It is unlikely that
the motor was manufactured at Hayes, as the case
is too shallow to house a Hayes made double spring
motor. It used a no. 23 soundbox.

His Master's Voice Model 301 *(c.1956)*

The Transportable (second version)

This model was described in 1956 as 'an ultra
modern successor to that justly famous model 113.'
The gramophone in the same advertisement
claims the model to be both a table grand model
and a transportable gramophone! As the author
has never come across an example, the model is
only included on the basis that it is a 'transportable'.
Whether the successor to the model 113 or not, if
this turns out not to have a carrying handle, it is
not a portable gramophone! The jury is out on this
one. The gramophone had a 10-inch turntable,
exponential horn, 5B soundbox, double spring
motor, walnut veneer with 'anodised gold grill'.

His Master's Voice Model 302 *(c.1957)*

This was a standard black model based on the 300
with a single spring motor and was only available
in black.

His Master's Voice De-Luxe Model 303 *(c.1957)*

The model appears to be the same as model 300.

101

Top left: Model 301 open.
Top right: Model 300 open.
Left: Model 118 open.
Above: Model 94 open.

THE
WORLD'S
FINEST
GRAMOPHONES
"His Master's Voice"

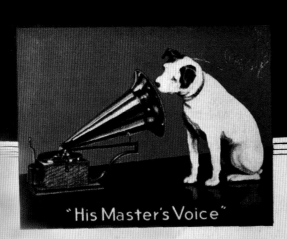

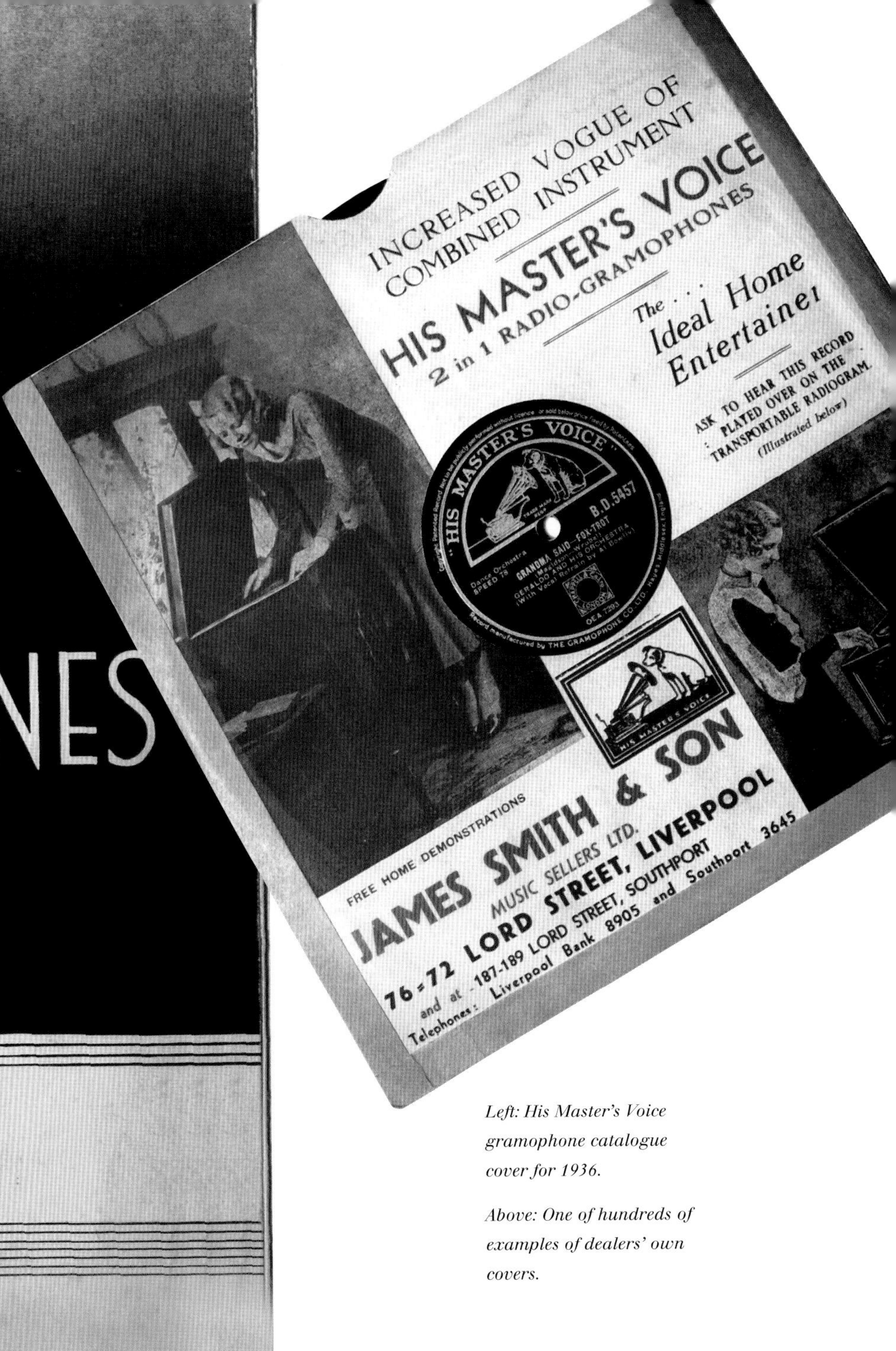

INCREASED VOGUE OF
COMBINED INSTRUMENT
HIS MASTER'S VOICE
2 in 1 RADIO-GRAMOPHONES
The . . .
Ideal Home
Entertainer
ASK TO HEAR THIS RECORD
PLAYED OVER ON THE
TRANSPORTABLE RADIOGRAM
(Illustrated below)
"HIS MASTER'S VOICE"
B.D.5457
GRANDMA SAID—FOX-TROT
GERALDO AND HIS ORCHESTRA
HIS MASTER'S VOICE
FREE HOME DEMONSTRATIONS
JAMES SMITH & SON
MUSIC SELLERS LTD.
76-72 LORD STREET, LIVERPOOL
and at 187-189 LORD STREET, SOUTHPORT
Telephones: Liverpool Bank 8905 and Southport 3645

Left: His Master's Voice gramophone catalogue cover for 1936.

Above: One of hundreds of examples of dealers' own covers.

Part 11
Collector's Tips.

How to date His Master's Voice instruments

His Master's Voice started using a system of dating manufacture on ivorine model identification plates attached to various products. These included items from irons to gramophones, radios etc. Some of the following portable models fell into this coding system, particularly the 102 and the later model 97.

The coding on the plates shows the year of manufacture starting from B (1936), B1 (1937), B2 (1938), B3 (1939), etc. (B6, 7, 8 were probably not used because of War production).

How to clean and repair portable gramophones

Portable gramophones are still relatively easy to find, especially black versions. Dealers who also restore gramophones tell me that nowadays they are less likely to scrap machines that, with a little extra effort, can be restored.

Because I am a restorer, I regard a machine that is in poor condition to be a challenge. With some effort and patience, I have achieved some pleasing results.

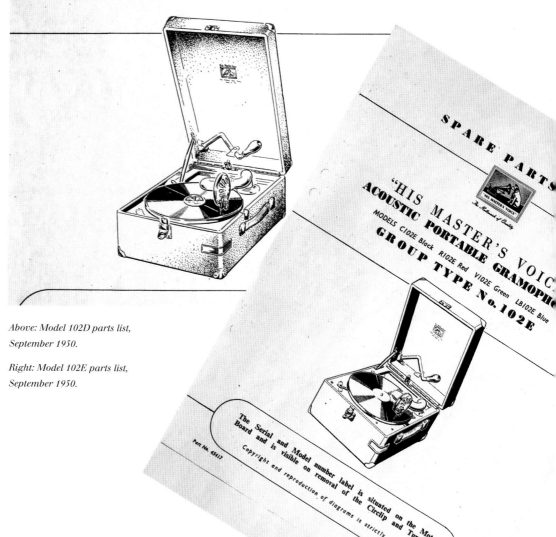

SPARE PARTS LIST

MODELS
C
R
V
LB

The Hallmark of Quality

"HIS MASTER'S VOICE"
ACOUSTIC PORTABLE GRAMOPHONES
MODELS C102D Black   R102D Red   V102D Green   LB102D Blue
GROUP TYPE No. 102D

Above: Model 102D parts list, September 1950.

Right: Model 102E parts list, September 1950.

SPARE PARTS

"HIS MASTER'S VOICE"
ACOUSTIC PORTABLE GRAMOPHO
MODELS C102E Black   R102E Red   V102E Green   LB102E Blue
GROUP TYPE No. 102E

The Serial and Model number label is situated on the Motor Board and is visible on removal of the Circlip and Turntable

Part No. 45417

Copyright and reproduction of diagrams is strictly reserved

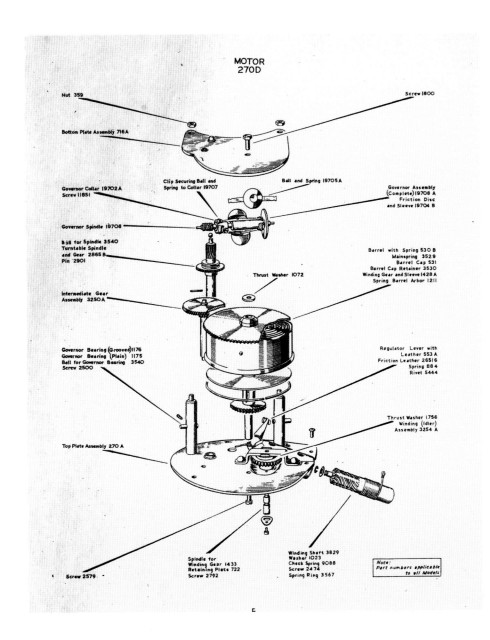

MOTOR
270D

Nut 359

Screw 1800

Bottom Plate Assembly 716A

Clip Securing Ball and
Spring to Collar 19707

Ball and Spring 19705A

Governor Collar 19702A
Screw 11851

Governor Assembly
(Complete) 19708 A
Friction Disc
and Sleeve 19704 B

Governor Spindle 19706

Ball for Spindle 3540
Turntable Spindle
and Gear 2865 B
Pin 2901

Thrust Washer 1072

Barrel with Spring 530 B
Mainspring 3529
Barrel Cap 531
Barrel Cap Retainer 3530
Winding Gear and Sleeve 1428 A
Spring Barrel Arbor 1211

Intermediate Gear
Assembly 3250A

Governor Bearing (Grooved) 1176
Governor Bearing (Plain) 1175
Ball for Governor Bearing 3540
Screw 2500

Regulator Lever with
Leather 553 A
Friction Leather 26516
Spring 884
Rivet 5444

Thrust Washer 1756
Winding (Idler)
Assembly 3254 A

Top Plate Assembly 270 A

Spindle for
Winding Gear 1433
Retaining Plate 722
Screw 2792

Winding Shaft 3829
Washer 1023
Check Spring 9088
Screw 2474
Spring Ring 3567

Note:
Part numbers applicable
to all Models

Screw 2579

Model 102E motor assembly.

Learning to restore gramophones is a fulfilling part of the hobby. I recall the pride (and relief!) I felt when I removed, cleaned and replaced my first mainspring.

Cleaning the case

Generally, portable gramophones are covered with durable leather-cloth which may need cleaning and/or repairing, especially on the outside of the case. Ensure that no areas to be cleaned are covered in paper of a similar appearance to cloth. Most machines were subject to smoke from open fires and from smokers. Remember, a gramophone may have had years of exposure to damp in a loft or garage since it was last regularly used, so the dirt it has acquired can be difficult to clean off.

It is best to remove all metal parts such as corner shields, escutcheons, locks, catches etc. before you start work. Be careful when unscrewing metal parts. Screws, untouched since the original assembly may be affected by rust and resist removal. Personally, before I start to clean a 101 machine both inside and out, I like to remove the record pocket.

The metal parts should clean up with polish. I prefer the chrome cleaner paste you buy from car accessory shops. This will be too harsh for some metal work, so use something less abrasive if you have any doubts. Be careful not to get over zealous and remove nickel or chrome plate! Rusted screws and clips may need wire brushing or rubbing with abrasive papers of different grades. Some restorers prefer to use fine wire wool, as it tends to reduce scratching. Re-nickeling or re-chroming of parts is a possibility, but you may have to save several items to be treated at the same time to make it a viable proposition. The alternatives are to leave any bare metal as it is (hopefully any remaining plate will have been protected during the cleaning process), or coat the bare metal with clear varnish.

Frankly, I would not advise the latter, and I only mention it because I know that some people carry out this treatment to retard the corrosive process. Varnish invariably ages poorly on metal and will craze and flake away. In my view it is not worth the effort.

Locks and catches are often rusted and need a lot of attention. Usually, I

Model 102E cabinet and fittings assembly.

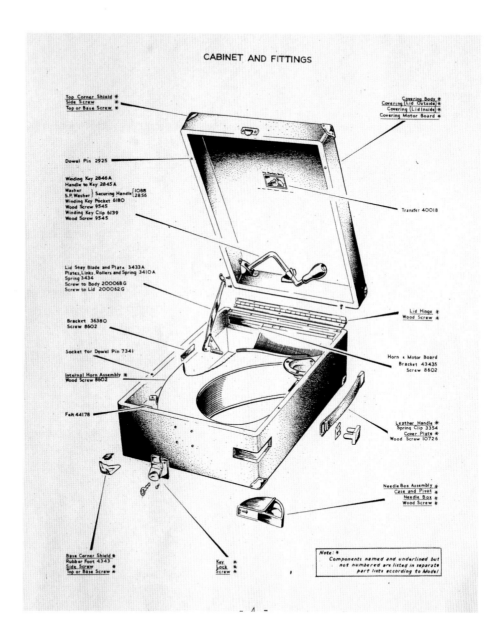

CABINET AND FITTINGS

squirt penetrating oil like, WD40, into a lock before starting. Keys can be made or found. So far, I have only found one lock broken and it was easy to find a replacement. Locks on portables were there mainly to keep the lids closed in transit. (You may acquire a machine without the top or bottom part of the lock where someone locked the lid and lost the key.) I prefer to make replacement keys if they are missing and although I am not an expert key cutter, one can usually find an old key that can be filed down to operate the locks on portables. It is helpful if you can borrow a key to use as a guide, but note that all locks and keys are not the same – just similar. Original keys that I have for portables have no Gramophone Company, His Master's Voice, or other identifying marks. As mentioned earlier, these were bought in from outside manufacturers.

Transfers should be avoided in the cleaning process as they can easily become brittle and will start to flake. A damaged transfer is a disappointing feature on an old gramophone.

Black machines can be brightened up after cleaning with black shoe polish applied carefully with a cloth or brush and polished off with a brush, followed

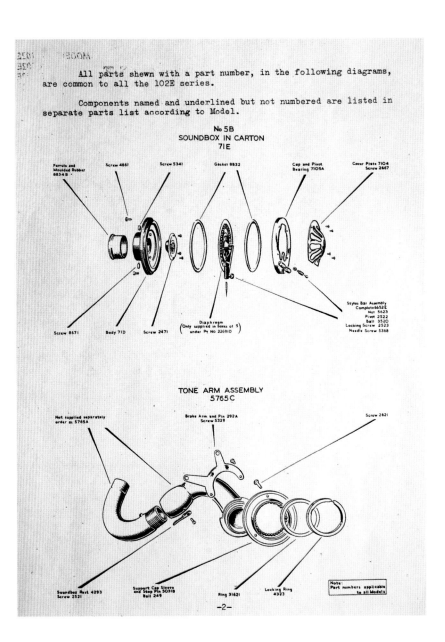

by a duster. Results are surprisingly good.

Coloured machines require more work and care. You need to determine the original colour by removing the metal corner shields or examining the inside of the case. Some books recommend the use of heavily coloured renovating polishes to smarten up cases. In my view this should be the last resort. I advocate cleaning the case, using neutral polish to smarten up the leather-cloth and thus maintaining its originality.

A case with the odd dent or mark or one with little chips out of the leather-cloth is acceptable. If a case is badly damaged, don't buy the gramophone! Such machines are suitable only as a source of spare parts for future projects.

I would never fully re-cover a case, although new leather-cloth is available in black. Small damaged areas can be re-covered using pieces carefully cut from overlapping cloth under the motor-board and glued in place. (Old record cases in bad condition are a good source of leather-cloth for repairs like these.) The cleaning and polishing process can then start.

Only where a turntable felt is either missing or in a dreadful state should it be replaced. Careful brushing of the dirty

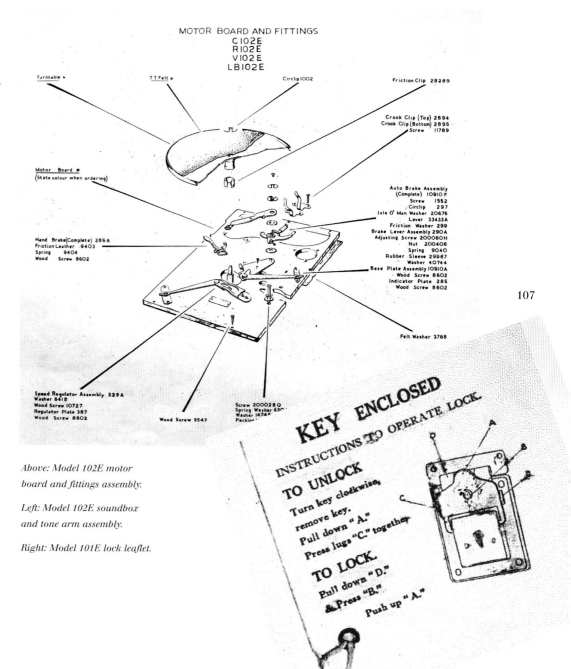

Above: Model 102E motor board and fittings assembly.

Left: Model 102E soundbox and tone arm assembly.

Right: Model 101E lock leaflet.

felt can restore it to a reasonable state. In my view a machine should be kept as original as possible.

Repairing soundboxes and motors
Motors
If you wish to maintain your own gramophones there are societies across the world, whose membership include people with both the technical knowledge and experience to help you. To avoid injury I strongly advise you to seek advice before you start. Let an expert show you how to safely carry out maintenance or repair mainsprings. *BE WARNED!*

I can recommend the City of London Phonograph and Gramophone Society, who publish quarterly a quality magazine. It has an international membership with branches across the United Kingdom who meet regularly. Through the magazine you will be able to contact societies in other countries including the United States, Australia and New Zealand. The society will also be able to advise you on likely sources of spare parts such as springs, mica diaphragms, gasket rings, needles and other items. Visit the website at *www.clpgs.org.uk* for details.

Right: 'The Portable Accompanist', The Voice 1930.

Whilst a number of motors are listed against the various models in this book, the most commonly found motors are as follows (with related mainspring types):-

Model	Motor	Spring size
100	400 series (425)	25 x 0.55 x 2745mm 1" wide x approx. 9' 2" long
101	400 series	As above
101	No. 59	25 x 0.55 x 4270mm 1" wide x approx. 14' 5" long
102	270 series	As above
99	23B	Check with your supplier
97	700 series 748; 794C etc	25 x 0.55 x 2745mm 1" wide x approx. 9' 2" long

As discussed earlier there were a number of other motors made during the production of certain models. Therefore, it is advisable to check with your supplier before ordering a mainspring, to ensure you have identified the correct item using the model number and any numbers shown on the base plate of the motor. Some suppliers will fit new springs for a small charge.

Soundboxes

If a mica (Exhibition or no. 4) soundbox rattles or buzzes noisily, it needs attention. The rubber gaskets on either face of the mica diaphragm often turn brittle and harden with age. The deterioration also causes general loss in sound quality as the diaphragm cannot vibrate and move freely. Damage like tears or lamination of the mica could cause problems. I recall a clumsy school friend accidentally putting his finger through a mica diaphragm.

To check the state of the gaskets, these soundboxes may be opened by removing the screws on the back plate. Usually, a sharp (but not excessive) tap on the end of a screwdriver whilst on the head of the screw is required to free the small brass screws. Once opened you can examine the gasket. If the rubber is still quite soft, you may wish to leave well alone. If it is hard and dried out, you may order a replacement. The mica diaphragm can be spoiled with careless handling, so again, you should seek help before attempting to replace dried out rubber gaskets.

Soundbox	Gasket ring size
Exhibition	43mm
No. 4	54mm

Undoing screws holding the soundbox together can also be problematic. Sometimes they will unscrew relatively easily using a precision screwdriver. Frustratingly though, particularly where a machine has spent its life in damp surroundings, one or more of the screws may refuse to budge. You may wish to try lubricating the screw for a period using WD40. However, there is no guarantee that this will work, in which case you may decide not to continue or seek advice before risking damage to the soundbox. Use penetrating oil sparingly. Too much and it may seep into the layers of the mica and cause damage.

Once you have removed the screws, the back plate may refuse to come off! Occasionally, the gasket ring attaches itself to the back plate and needs careful detachment. Other times the back plate is simply stuck. The Exhibition and early no.4 soundboxes were made from a brass base, (blackened on the back), and a nickel-plated brass front. Both plates of these soundboxes, held together with screws, are generally strong enough to be repaired. First, the brass back plate on the no. 4 box, then the front, was replaced by an alloy, which over time may become brittle and therefore better left alone.

I would seek advice or again, stop the process as it could crack or break if force is applied. If in doubt ask an expert for advice.

The metal fronted no. 5a and no. 5b soundboxes suffer from the same problem of being fitted with a die-cast back plate. The no. 16 soundbox was not designed for repair. It was pressed together rather than held by screws. The only cure for a bad no. 16 soundbox is a replacement. Never heat die castings, they may explode.

There may be other problems; stiff stylus bar mountings may need adjusting. This can result in severe wear to your 78-rpm records. A loose stylus bar will cause rattling during reproduction.

In conclusion, unless you know what you are doing, leave repairs of motors and soundboxes to experts, or get advice first.

Broken parts

Broken parts are obviously problematical. Usually, dealers have stocks of parts taken from scrapped machines and new reproduction parts like rubber gasket rings for no. 4 soundboxes and rubber backs for Exhibition soundboxes.

It is common for winding handle clips to be broken. You may have difficulty obtaining original parts. There are other solutions; make your own replacement parts or contact specialists from the phone book in your own area. A local shoe repairer makes replacement leather carrying handles for me.

Missing parts

Missing parts are a headache. A machine may have any amount of parts missing, but most common amongst them are:

The turntable circlip

The turntable circlip removed to take off the turntable to lubricate the motor. If this is not replaced, the turntable will revolve (or try to) when the machine is carried or stored on its side. The circlip holds the turntable in place so that brakes are properly engaged. A temporary solution is to push a paper clip over the centre spindle.

The record album on model 99s

Record dealers are most likely to have these as they ended up with the rest of an owner's record collection and not replaced on the machine. The 99 albums were made specifically for the machine and others are not good replacements. I have seen only one model 99 with the record album still attached.

This beach scene appeared on many record covers.
The man lies back while a friend does all the work!

Poor Nipper

Poor Nipper goes 'walkies' from some portable machines. I have seen a number of 101s without the record pocket where the trademark would normally be. Even the plaque in the lid of the 102 can go missing. At least two coloured 102s have passed my way in this condition. I have even seen a black 102 plaque for sale in a frame at a collector's fair! Considering how easy it is to find a His Master's Voice trademark if you really want one, and how small transfers are on machines, it seems to be a wasteful way of working.

Replacement record pockets and plaques can be expensive as they come from machines that are dismantled for parts. A gramophone minus its trade transfer should cost less, therefore this extra expense may be a good investment.

Why choose a His Master's Voice portable machine?

Why, when there were so many other makes of portable gramophone during the clockwork era, should the His Master's Voice portable still be so popular with collectors? The fact is the trademark is still a well-loved image and a sign of a quality product. People have affection for 'the dog'. Some like me had an example in the house during their early years (often a model 101). The large numbers sold during production and a high survival rate has kept prices reasonable. This compares with genuine horn models which in the right condition can bring a steep price – if you can get your hands on one! Other makes, some of which were good quality machines, are often passed over for a His Master's Voice model.

Advantages

Models 101 and 102 are outstanding both in style and performance. The sound reproduction and general reliability is at least comparable with most other portable machines. You can carry them around, demonstrate them to your friends and store them away easily afterwards.

Nowadays, old portable gramophones are less expensive than other models, although coloured machines may prove costly depending on rarity or desirability.

As mentioned earlier, spares for most models are not hard to find. Soundboxes can be a problem though, especially if good replacements for no. 16, 5a, and 5b are required. An original chrome no. 4 soundbox for a late 101 is not likely to have survived in excellent condition. (Front and back are both castings). You still get that great gramophone smell – a cocktail of metal, wood, oil, grease and polish.

Disadvantages

Record damage caused by poor storage. The model 99 was the only His Master's Voice portable providing minimal care for the fragile 78 with a record album. Other machines mentioned, encouraged the storage of records without covers when not in use, in record pockets or trays. I cannot be the only one who gets frustrated with badly scuffed records.

Except for the first His Master's Voice machine, you can't close the lid when playing your records on most portables, therefore you are prone to needle chatter. Trying to close the lid before putting the soundbox into the storage position causes the familiar needle scarring inside the lid covering. Although the no.4 soundbox is cut for fibre needles, it is not very effective. The no. 16 is better, lighter and more compliant.

When properly designed, the larger the horn, the better the air column loading of the soundbox and therefore there is less resistance at the needle point. Portable gramophones cause more record wear, especially on bass notes.

Glossary

Escutcheon
The protective plate around the opening or hole in the case for the winding handle (or winding 'key').

Ferrule
A metal ring inserted into the record pocket (in the lid of a portable) which fits around the turntable spindle when closed.

Ivorine
Celluloid used for the manufacture of identifying plates on gramophones.

Mica
Transparent mineral material used for the diaphragm of soundboxes. (Models 100 and 101 in this instance – Exhibition and no. 4 soundboxes).

Pocket
Record storage compartment usually in the lid of a portable gramophone (eg. model 101).

Shield
Metal corner used to protect outer cases.

Tropical models
Different versions of the portable models for the Indian market, presumably, to avoid the problems of extreme humidity, with solid teak cases preferred to leather-cloth. On model 102s, various banding designs appeared in the case. The cases and lines were painted in various colours.

Tungstyle
Long lasting gramophone needle made by The Gramophone Co, invented in the USA and sold there under the name 'Tungstone'. They consisted of a tungsten wire set in a brass shank.

Winding key
Winding handle.

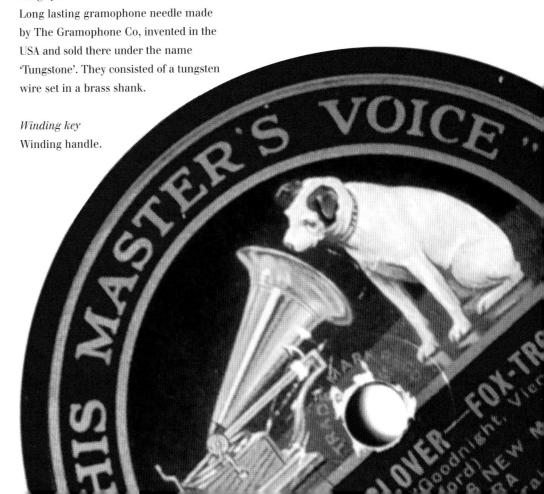

List of parts illustrated and referred to in the text

Parts lists would be useful (if commonly available) to allocate the correct parts to a model requiring attention. I have included drawings of fittings including winding keys (also referred to as 'winding handles' or 'cranks'), locks, catches, ferrules and others found on His Master's Voice portable gramophones. Standard finishes were used on parts, but some terms describing them varied on parts lists.

The parts appear 50% of actual size, to assist restorers. Photocopy the pages at 200% to return them to actual size. A summary is shown below: -

Bl.	Black
CHR PL; CHR; Ch.P; CP	All refer to Chrome Plating
PF BN; PF; BN; Par. B; OB	Parkerised Finish Black Nickel
	[Believed to be another name for Oxidised Blackening (OB)]
NG	Nickel Gloss (Nickel Plating-polished)
WN	White Nickel (as above-unpolished)
EN	Enamel
Bl. En	Black Enamel
C.B.	Camera Black
Std.	Standard

Some parts lists used number codes instead to describe finishes.

You will find numbers given in the text when reference is made to a particular part used on a machine. Descriptions of these are shown in the table below with the drawings of each on the following pages.

Ref no.
Gramophone Model
Part Description

1

100; 101; 102
Ferrule.

2

100
Lid catch. Style 1.

3

100; 101A-J
Winding handle clip.

4

100; 101A; 99
Winding handle escutcheon
Style 1.

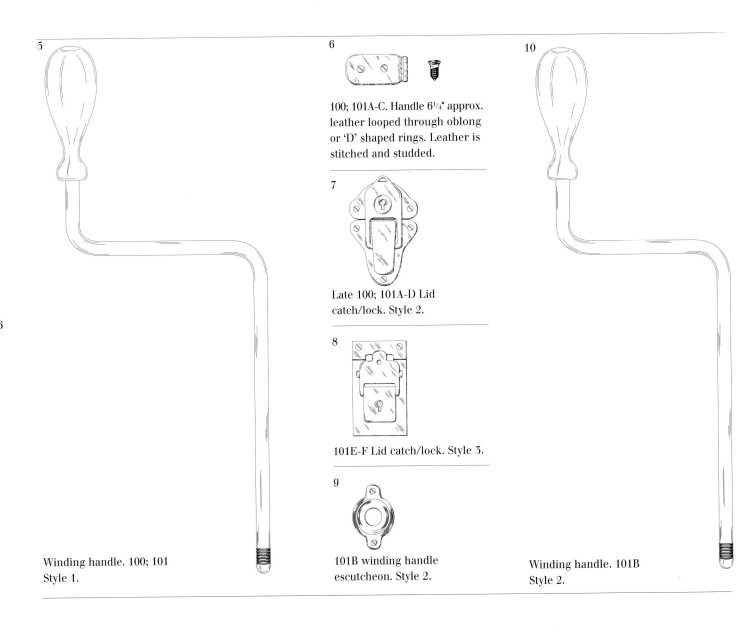

5

Winding handle. 100; 101
Style 1.

6

100; 101A-C. Handle 6¼" approx.
leather looped through oblong
or 'D' shaped rings. Leather is
stitched and studded.

7

Late 100; 101A-D Lid
catch/lock. Style 2.

8

101E-F Lid catch/lock. Style 3.

9

101B winding handle
escutcheon. Style 2.

10

Winding handle. 101B
Style 2.

11

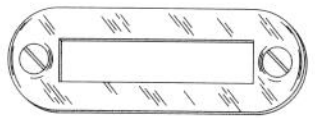

101B-C tungstyle needle tin clip. Style 1.

12

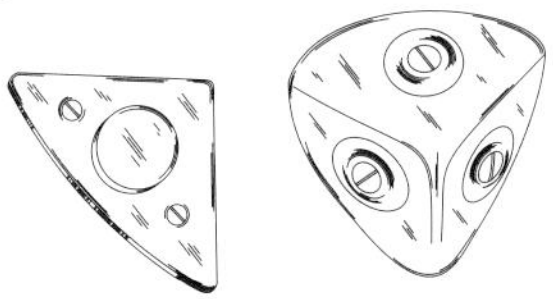

100; 101 case corners. (Bottom corners with rubber studs from 101B).

13

101C winding handle escutcheon. Style 3.

14

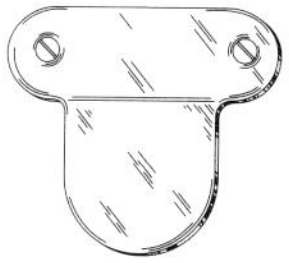

101C winding handle escutcheon covering plate.

15

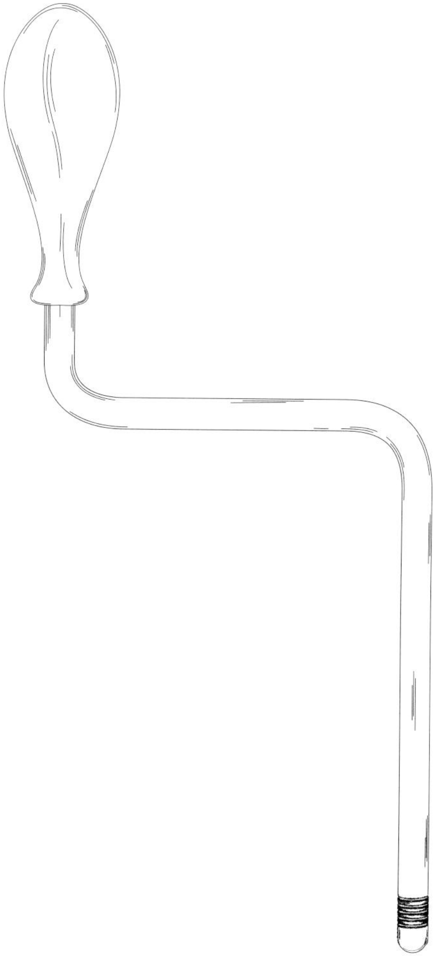

101C-N winding handle Style 3.

18

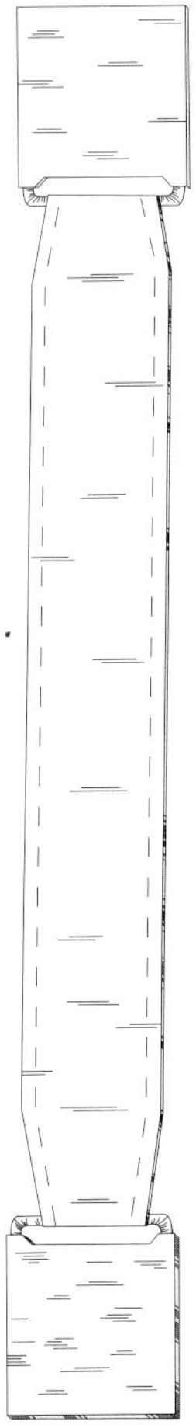

Style 2. Pakana carrying handle.

16

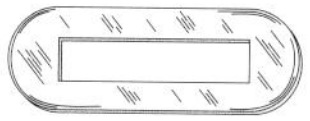

101C onwards tungstyle needle tin clip. Style 2.

17

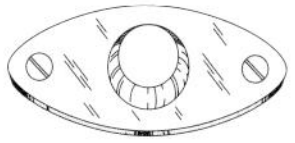

101D winding handle escutcheon Style 4. Protruding eye directs winding handle to motor, usually with single winding handle guiding plate. (See 19 top)

19

Single

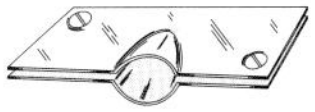

Double

Single & double winding handle to motor guiding plates.

20

101E-F ivorine identifying plate. Style 1.

21

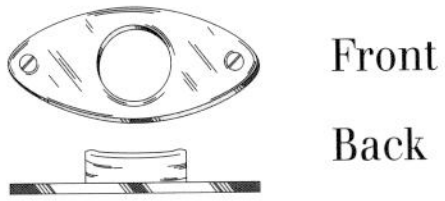

Front

Back

101G (later versions); 101H-L
Winding handle escutcheon
Style 5.

25

Lid catch/lock. Style 5.

29

Tungstyle needle clip tin Style 4.
Appeared only briefly on 102s.

33

Lid catch/lock Style 7.

22

THE GRAMOPHONE CO LTD
MODEL
101
No
136865
HAYES MIDDLESEX ENGLAND

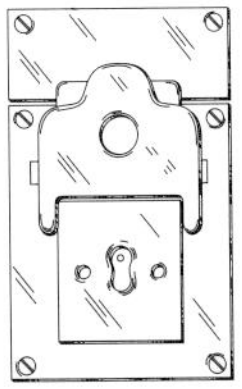

101G ivorine identifying plate
Style 2.

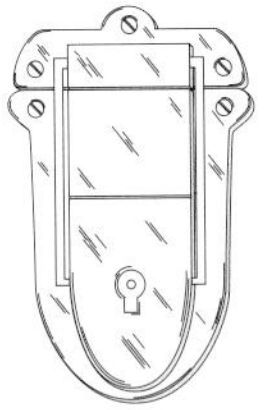

26

Lid catch/lock. Style 6.

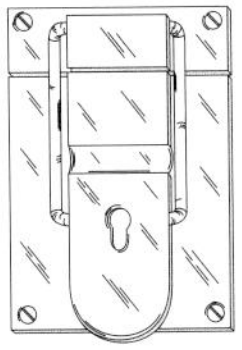

30

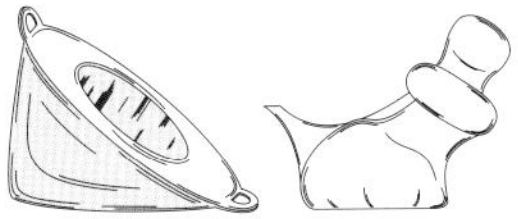

Improved, stronger winding
handle clip and socket.

34

REF TO THIS INSTRUMENT
QUOTE MODEL 102C
SERIAL NO. 534961

102; 97; post-1936 models,
ivorine identifying plate.
Style 4.

23

FOR SPARES
QUOTE
GIOIG

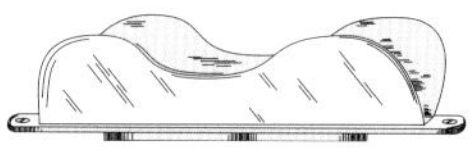

Later 101G-J metal identifying
plate. (Metal version 1)

27

FOR SPARES QUOTE
POUR LES PIECES DE
RECHANGE CITER
FÜR ERSATZTEILE
BITTE ANKGEBEN
VIOIJ

Metal tri-language identifying
plate. (Metal version 2)

31

MODEL 101
QUOTE No
1010014544
IN CORRESPONDENCE
CONCERNING
THIS MACHINE

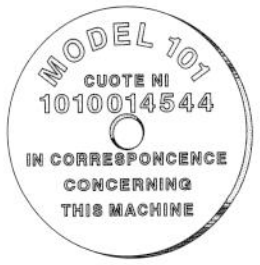

101K-L Early 102s; 99 ivorine
identifying plate Style 3.

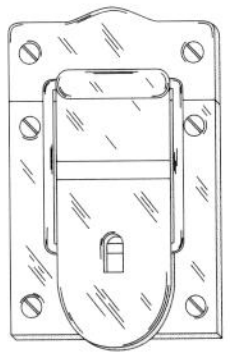

35

102A-E winding handle
escutcheon. Style 7.

24

Lid catch/lock. Style 4.

28

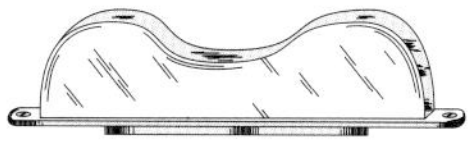

101J-L; 102A-H; 99 tungstyle
needle clip tin Style 3.

32

101M-N winding handle
escutcheon Style 6.

36

SLOW   FAST

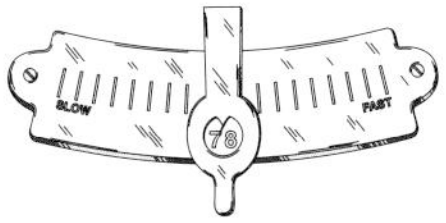

101; 102 Speed indicator plate
Version 1.

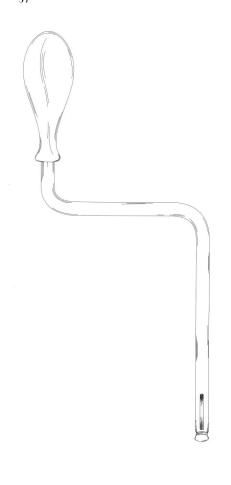

99 speed indicator plate
Version 2.

43

39

99 winding handle clip
& socket.

42
99 winding handle Style 5.

43
97 winding handle Style 6.

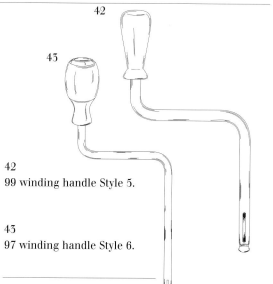

40

99 case corners.

44

97 speed indicator plate
Version 3.

41

102 winding handle. Style 4.

99 lid catch/lock. Style 8.

45

97 winding handle escutcheon
Style 8.

A selection of the more commonly found motors on HMV portable gramophones.

1. Model 100; motor (400 series/410 side wind. Note the flat governor weights.
2. Model 101; motor (400 series/410 side wind. Note the bottom plate required to be 'trimmed' to fit into the case; the governor weights are rounded.
3. Model 101; motor no. 59, encased, with longer mainspring than the 400 series.
4. Model 99; motor no. 23b.
5. Model 102; typical 270 series motor.

1

2

3

4

5

Advertisements from Punch magazine.
Left: *23 December 1925*, centre: *17 July 1929*,
right: *18 July 1928*.

Index

FAVOURITE HITS FROM THE PORTABLE YEARS

1. **Stevedore Stomp** Duke Ellington & his Cotton Club Orch. B6106. New York. 7/3/29
2. **Painting the Clouds with Sunshine** Gracie Fields. B3291. 9/1/30
3. **Limehouse Blue**s Jack Hylton & his Orch. B5789. London.10/1/30
4. **You Forgot Your Gloves** Jack Buchanan. B4005. 29/10/31
5. **Grasshopper's Dance** Jack Hylton & his Orch. B3790. London. 16 June 1931
6. **Mad Dogs and Englishmen** Noel Coward. B4269. 20/9/32
7. **Dancing in the Dark** Ambrose & his Orch. (Voc. Sam Browne). B6132. 11/1/32
8. **West End Blues** Louis Armstrong & his Hot Five. Parlophone. R448. Chicago. 28/6/28
9. **Echo of a Song** Ray Noble & his New Mayfair Dance Orch. (Voc. Al Bowlly). B6193. London. 8/6/32
10/11. **Our Village Concert 1 & 2** Sydney Howard, Vera Pearce, Leonard Henry & Co. C1782. 15/10/29
12. **Bach Goes to Town** Benny Goodman & his Orch. B8879. 15/12/38
13. **My Last Year's Girl** Jack Hulbert (with Eddie & Rex). B8162 London. 9/3/34
14. **Wedding Of The Painted Doll** Jack Hylton & his Orch. (Voc. Sam Browne). B5637 London. 26/4/29
15. **Nasty Man** Ray Noble & his Orch. (Voc. Dorothy Carless). B6499. London. 28/6/32
16. **On a Cold and Frosty Morning** Ray Noble & his New Mayfair Dance Orch. B6097. London. 14/11/31
17. **I Guess I'll Have to Change My Plan** Ambrose & his Orch. (Voc. Sam Browne). B6261. 18/10/32
18. **April In Paris** Artie Shaw & his Orch. B9105. 13/5/40
19. **They Say** Geraldo & his Orch. (Voc. Al Bowlly). B5448. London. 10/1/39
20. **Stardust** Ambrose & his Orch. B5967. 19/1/31